WITHDRAWN

The Beginner's Guide to
Preserving
Food at Home

Janet Chadwick

Storey Publishing

*The mission of Storey Publishing is to serve our customers by
publishing practical information that encourages
personal independence in harmony with the environment.*

Edited by Margaret Sutherland and Cindy Littlefield
Art direction and book design by Mary Winkelman Velgos
Cover design by Alethea Morrison
Text production by Liseann Karandisecky

Cover and interior decorative illustrations by © Kate Quinby, Croak & Hum
How-to illustrations by Elayne Sears

Expert reader: Elizabeth L. Andress, Extension Food Safety Specialist Director, National
    Center for Home Food Preservation Department of Foods and Nutrition
Indexed by Christine R. Lindemer, Boston Road Communications

Recipe on page 140 was previously published in *Keeping the Harvest*, by Nancy Chioffi and
Gretchen Mead (Storey Publishing).
    Recipe on page 157 was previously published in *Weekend!*, by Edith Stovel and Pamela
Wakefield (Storey Publishing).

Printed in the United States by Versa Press
10 9 8 7 6 5 4 3 2 1

Library of Congress Cataloging-in-Publication Data

Chadwick, Janet, 1933–
  The beginner's guide to preserving food at home / by Janet Bachand Chadwick.
      p. cm.
  Previous ed. published under title: Busy person's guide to preserving food, 1995.
  Includes index.
  ISBN 978-1-60342-145-4 (pbk. : alk. paper)
  1. Food—Preservation. I. Chadwick, Janet, 1933–
  Busy person's guide to preserving food. II. Title.
TX601.C43 2009
641.4—dc22
                              2009006688

Contents

Acknowledgments

I would like to thank Louellan Wasson, home economist, for her technical editing and moral support throughout the writing of this book. Many others deserve thanks, too: Andrea Chesman, my editor, who had the original idea for this book; Mary Clark of Garden Way, for obtaining many new items of food processing equipment for me to test; Moulinex and General Electric companies, in particular Mr. Ted Miller of General Electric Co., for making available to me food processors for testing; Lynn Liberty of Garden Way Living Center, for her never-failing support; Win Way, University of Vermont Extension Agronomist, for his educated palate; and Elayne Sears for her descriptive illustrations.

Last but not least, I'd like to thank my family, especially my husband, Raymond, for taking on extra gardening chores to help make this book possible, and to my daughter, Kim, for her all-around help.

For this revised edition, the publishers thank Elizabeth L. Andress, Ph.D., Professor and Extension Food Safety Specialist Director at the National Center for Home Food Preservation at the University of Georgia. Her thorough review of the book was invaluable. And thanks, also, to Cindy Littlefield, who incorporated the updates without changing the appealing simplicity of the original text.

The Busy Person's Dilemma

YOU HAVE THREE CHILDREN UNDER FIVE, the baby cried all night, and your mother-in-law is coming for supper. What are you going to do with that bushel of green beans? Or, it's Thursday, and you just arrived home after a hard day at the office. You know that if you wait until Saturday to make dill pickles, the cucumbers will be too large; but if you pick them now, they will be punky by Saturday . . . but you don't feel like pickling until midnight. What are you going to do? Well, take a deep breath and relax. This book is for you.

Vegetable gardening is rapidly becoming the number one American pastime. Escalating food costs, inferior quality products, and aversions to chemical additives have convinced many of us that the best way to provide our families with good food at reasonable costs is to raise it ourselves.

When calculating the savings of a garden and home food processing, many people (always nongardeners) will remark, "Yes, but how much is your time worth?" To answer that question you have to be honest with yourself. Would you really be holding down an extra job during those hours that would net you more cash in the bank? Can you put a price tag on the physical, emotional, and spiritual satisfactions that you derive from working the soil and producing the foods that nourish your family? Is the kind of food you feed your family important to you? Is there any way you can buy the feeling of pride you have at the sight of the full freezer; the rows of canned vegetables, fruits, pickles, jams, and jellies; or the root cellar shelves filled to the ceiling? If these things are not important to you, then maybe you should not be gardening or preserving food, because there *is* a lot of work involved — but the work should be a joy and a challenge to your ability to be more self-reliant.

I've written this book for those of you who garden and hold down outside jobs or are busy with kids and other outside activities. I know that it is hard enough to cope with the normal routine of family, home, and job, along with raising a small garden for fresh summer vegetables, without trying to squeeze in long hours of food preservation at the end of a busy day. But much food can be preserved for storage in the small blocks of time you have available on a daily or weekly basis. This book can be used as a primer if you are new to the art of food preservation, and it's likely to provide new and exciting ideas to those of you who have been preserving food for years.

How Can This Book Help You?

FREEZING IS THE MOST POPULAR METHOD of food preservation. It's a great time-saving method, and it produces the best finished product; and so this book will focus strongly on freezing techniques, including some new methods that are even more efficient and produce an even better finished product.

Drying is an ancient method of preserving food, one that is gaining in popularity as people discover how much they enjoy having an inexpensive supply of gourmet Italian dried tomatoes and kid-pleasing fruit leathers. Also, as more and more people grow their own herbs, they find drying a convenient way of preserving that harvest. So I will offer plenty of advice for drying fruits, vegetables, and herbs.

I will also discuss the equipment that is absolutely necessary for food preservation and provide information on other equipment that, while not absolutely required, will make food preservation faster, easier, and in general, result in a better finished product.

For people who are serious about food preservation, I will talk about steps that can be taken year-round to make harvest time easier. Throughout the book, you will find tips to help you make the best use of weekends, weekdays, and overnight hours. These tips will include the best times to harvest vegetables as well as the best ways to keep them fresh for up to three days, so that you can plan to harvest one day and preserve a day or so later.

Since I can already hear nutritionists raising their voices in a collective uproar over this last remark, I think I'd better explain myself. Many commercially sold fresh vegetables and fruits are treated with chemicals to preserve their *look* of freshness; they can be from two days to two weeks old when they appear in your market. You have no way of knowing how many times frozen foods have been defrosted and refrozen (losing nutrients and flavor) before they show up in the frozen food cases of your market. Nor is there any way to judge the hours or days that lapsed between the harvest and processing of canned foods. You will never know what chemicals were sprayed on these foods while they were growing.

Taking those factors into consideration, preserving homegrown foods lets you start out ahead of the game. Even though the *best* way to preserve all the nutrients and fresh flavor of foods is to pick them at their peak and process them immediately, you can be sure that waiting even two days between harvest and processing will not cost you much more than minimal loss of either nutrients or flavor *if you follow my instructions on storing.* Therefore, you have nothing to lose and everything to gain by preserving your food by my methods.

In addition to step-by-step, illustrated instructions for processing commonly grown vegetables and fruits, I've included recipes for ketchup, salsa, pickles, jams, jellies, and herbal vinegars. I've also shared ideas for delicious meals that can be prepared ahead of harvest time to make busy days much easier. Some of these dishes incorporate the vegetables being preserved. Finally, I've included a list of suppliers to help you equip your kitchen.

Before we get into serious food preservation, I'd like to share three important pieces of advice. First, make an effort to involve the whole family whenever practical so that everybody becomes excited about what you are accomplishing and the independence it can afford you. Second, stay flexible. This is important mostly from a psychological standpoint. If you become too rigid in your expectations, you will waste tremendous amounts of emotional energy trying to keep up, or being disappointed at failures. This approach can ruin the best of goals. Finally, know yourself. If you work best at night, plan your work for the evening hours; but if you are a morning person, get up an hour or so earlier in the morning to accomplish extra tasks.

The following pages are packed with information to help you make the best use of your time and resources during the harvest season. Good luck and have fun!

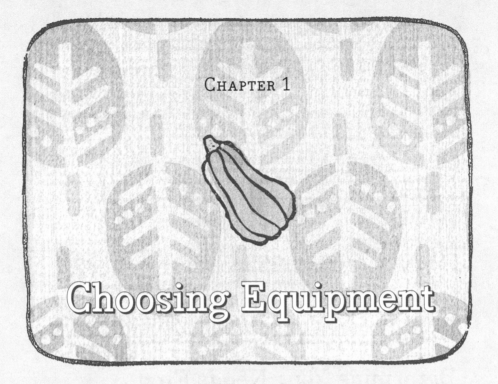

CHAPTER 1

Choosing Equipment

PEA SHELLERS, APPLE PEELERS, cherry pitters, food mills, food processors, microwave ovens: Are they really time-savers in the harvest kitchen?

If you are serious about making food preservation as quick and easy as possible, you will want to invest in some time-saving equipment. The right equipment not only makes work easier and more enjoyable, but the end results are usually better, so the feeling of satisfaction is greater.

YOU DO NOT NEED TO PURCHASE the most expensive equipment on the market; some very good and reliable products are sold at reasonable prices. A good food processor is just about the best helping hand a busy person can have at harvest time. Prices range from as low as $45 to around $200 for one of the best Cuisinart models with all the attachments. Once you realize what a help this type of appliance will be throughout the year, you will probably see it as a good investment.

On the other hand, not every new gadget advertised will be worth the money. In this chapter, I will concentrate on the food-processing items that I have tested and found useful in my kitchen.

Determine Your Needs First

BEFORE YOU STEP INTO A STORE or look through a catalog, you should have a good idea of just what equipment you need. This decision, of course, will depend on the foods you will prepare and the methods of preservation you will use. Will you freeze? Can? Pickle? Store in a root cellar? Dry? Will you need to chop? Slice? Dice? Grind? Purée?

If you haven't decided just how you will be preserving your harvest, glance ahead to chapters 3, 4, and 5 to assess which methods will best meet your needs. There is no point in investing in equipment you won't use.

BASIC EQUIPMENT LIST

For Root Cellaring

* boxes
* barrels
* large plastic bags
* crocks

For Freezing

* freezer
* scrub brush
* strainers (fine sieves and colanders)
* paring and chopping knives
* food processing equipment (grinders, slicers, blenders, or food processors)
* measuring cups and spoons
* widemouthed funnel
* timer
* hot pads, mitts, or heavy potholders
* towels
* large bowls
* large roaster or kettle
* cookie sheets or jelly roll pans
* freezer bags and containers

For Drying

Everything on the freezing list, plus a dehydrator or oven

For Canning in a Boiling-Water Bath

Everything on the freezing list plus:

* boiling-water-bath canner
* preserving kettle
* teakettle
* soup ladle
* nonmetallic spatula or wooden chopstick
* large wooden and slotted spoons
* jar lifter or tongs
* canning jars and lids

Choosing
Equipment

3

THE EXPENSIVE APPLIANCES

In my kitchen, I have found that I really save time by using my freezer, dishwasher, food processor, and microwave oven. Of course, you can preserve food without these appliances, but their year-round uses justify their costs.

Freezers

Although a freezer is a major investment, freezing is very often the fastest method of food processing, and it generally gives you a product that is closest to fresh.

Small freezers contained in refrigerators are not cold enough to freeze and store foods. Your freezer must be a separate unit that maintains a temperature of 0°F or lower to stop the growth of bacteria, yeasts, and molds. Temperatures this low will also greatly inhibit the enzyme action that can cause discoloration and destroy the fresh flavor of frozen foods.

Costs. When you buy a new freezer, research more than just the name-brand models and take their operating costs into consideration. New energy-efficient models cost much less per year to operate than older models, a consideration if you are contemplating a used freezer. Each new freezer should list the approximate amount of energy the unit consumes per year, so be sure to do some comparison shopping. Self-defrosting freezers may not cost more to operate than manual-defrosting models. Accumulated frost in a manual-defrosting model acts as an insulator between the cooling coils and the interior, so additional energy is required to keep the unit cold and to recool the entire freezer after it has been defrosted.

Chest Freezers Versus Upright Freezers. Chest freezers tend to be colder since cold air does not rise quickly when the lid is raised. They hold more food overall per cubic foot and usually cost less than upright models. Upright freezers use less floor space, and they make reaching for food more convenient. But cold air spills from them when the doors are opened; therefore, operating costs are greater.

Much of the space in an upright goes to waste since it must be packed so that food won't fall out when the door is opened.

Microwave Ovens

Microwaves perform many time-saving functions when it comes to preserving food. Where they really shine is in the preparation work for freezing — blanching vegetables and heating sugar syrups. They are also quite handy for cooking fruits before puréeing for fruit leathers. And, of course, microwaves are great for the year-round tasks of cooking fresh and frozen vegetables for the table and rehydrating dried foods.

Any microwave, however, is limited in its versatility, and it should not be used for making preserves or drying most foods, despite the recommendations of some people. Some books do include recipes for microwave preserves; these recipes usually work in quantities no greater than 4 cups of fruit. The cooking times are comparable to larger batches done on top of the stove, and the hot fruit mixture has a tendency to boil over the top of the cooking container and make a mess inside the oven. Also, a tremendous amount of steam is generated, which can be hazardous.

Microwave drying is not recommended by some oven manufacturers, as removing all of the moisture from the oven creates what's known as a "no-load" situation that can damage the machine's magnetron tube over time. Microwave drying can also cause a "volcanic effect." That is, the food feels very hot and dry on the outside but is still moist on the inside. If food is stored in this state, the moisture can turn into mold or cause the food to become rancid. In addition, the intensity of a microwave makes it very easy to overdry foods, resulting in a burned or charred flavor. Some foods, such as herbs, may even catch on fire.

So while drying foods in a microwave oven is possible, it is not always wise. Be sure to consult the manufacturer's instructions before attempting to use your microwave oven to dry foods or herbs.

Never use the microwave to sterilize jars for canning — it just doesn't do the job.

Dehydrators

Do you really need this extra piece of equipment? Well, no. But after a few seasons of drying food in your oven or air-drying above your woodstove or outside in the sun — if you live in a hot, dry, sunny climate — you may find that the ease of drying and the convenience of dried foods make drying your favorite method of preservation. Then it will be time to invest in this handy appliance. Dehydrators range in price from about $30 to more than $100.

Like other kitchen appliances, home food dehydrators come in an array of sizes, shapes, and colors, with a wide assortment of features. The basic components of an effective dehydrator include a heat source, a fan to circulate the heat and remove moist air, and trays for the food. Other desirable features include a thermostat to regulate the temperature from a low of about 100°F (for herbs) to a high of about 140°F (for meats) and a timer that will turn off the dehydrator.

When choosing a size, consider how much counter space you can allow for it during use and how much storage space you have when it is not in use. Also, consider how much drying space you want. As a rule of thumb, 12 square feet of drying area is sufficient for a half-bushel of vegetables.

Food Processors

Food processors work so fast that washing the vegetables, cutting them to size, and placing them in the feed tube takes more time than the actual processing. This versatile appliance combines many of the functions of the blender, grinder, and slicer. While processors do not purée as efficiently as blenders, they do a creditable job. They will also grind coffee and meat, and slice, julienne, shred, and grate. Many have accessories that will allow you to cut and ripple cut

French fries. They make breads, piecrusts, and sauces with just a flick of the wrist. They can be taken apart easily for cleaning, and most parts are dishwasher safe.

Which Food Processor to Buy. You can choose between two basic types of processors: direct-drive, which means that the bowl and blades sit directly on top of the motor's shaft; and belt-driven, where the bowl mounts to one side of the motor. The belt-driven types take up more counter space than the direct-drive processors, and the belt-driven machines that I have tested seem to overheat faster than those with direct-drive.

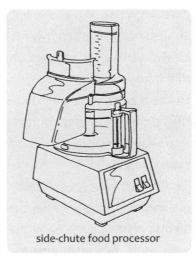

side-chute food processor

Most food processors feed the chopped, diced, or sliced vegetables into a bowl. The larger the bowl, the fewer times you will have to empty the vegetables into a larger bowl, and the less time your work will take.

Blenders, Strainers, Food Mills, and Other Useful (and Useless) Tools

Before the electric food processor, many electric and manual appliances made food processing easy. I still use my hand-cranked Squeezo strainer and wouldn't be without it. You may want to use a few of these appliances during the harvest season.

Blenders have become almost a standard appliance in most kitchens. They can be used to mince, chop, grate, purée, or just blend. They are not as efficient as food processors for coarsely chopping or grating vegetables, since they tend to chop too finely; however, they do a better job of puréeing than the food processor. Blenders often are easier to clean than food processors.

If you make your own tomato juice, sauce, or purée; make soup purées; freeze winter squash or pumpkins; or make your own applesauce, you will not want to be without a good **strainer or food mill** during the harvest season. Unlike blenders, they will minimize the amount of air incorporated into sauces and purées during processing.

blender

Three basic types of strainers and mills are available, but if you preserve large quantities of food, the best is the type that uses hand-cranked augers to crush the food and force it through perforated, cone-shaped strainers or screens. Large hoppers direct the purées into bowls, while augers move the skins, seeds, and cores into waste bowls at the other end. When using these strainers to process apples, just quarter and cook the fruit until tender. Tomatoes can be quartered and puréed uncooked. I can strain 7 quarts of tomato purée in just 10 minutes in my hand-cranked strainer, and the finished product is excellent.

These strainers are meant for large jobs, and they take a little extra time for cleanup. All parts can be washed in the dishwasher. The strainer screens, which are the hardest part to clean, can be cleaned quickly and easily by forcing a large canning jar scrub brush down inside the straining screen and giving it a few twists. Before

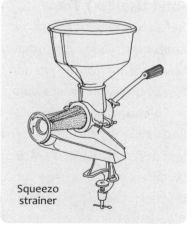

Squeezo strainer

removing the brush, scrub the outside of the screen with a small stiff-bristled brush.

The smaller **Foley food mill**, shaped like a 2-quart saucepan with holes in the bottom, has a handle with a horizontal cranking arm that operates a semicircular disk that forces the food through the holes. Underneath, a spring-loaded wire scrapes the bottom

food mill

clean. Releasing a nut on the bottom allows it to come apart easily for cleaning. The Foley Food Mill doesn't work efficiently on items with tough skins. For instance, tomato skins and seeds tend to get clogged in the bottom. By reversing the action of the disk, however, it can be unclogged quite easily, and you can either remove the skins or continue straining. Foley Food Mills are readily available wherever kitchenware is sold.

Chinois strainers — cone-shaped strainers with pestles — come in aluminum or stainless steel. A large wooden pestle, made to fit snugly in the bottom of the cone, presses food against the sides to squeeze it through. Tomato seeds are frequently forced through the holes, giving the tomato purée a speckled look. These strainers cost under $20.

For making clear fruit juices, you will need a jelly bag or cheese-cloth for straining out fruit pulp. These can be set inside a colander or strainer. (Cheesecloth is also needed to cover food that is being dried outside.)

A variety of manually operated vegetable and cabbage **slicers** on the market cost anywhere from a few dollars to under $50. While they can't possibly be as efficient as a food processor, they still pro-duce a nice product with less effort than slicing with a knife.

My food processor does such a good job of julienne-slicing beans with the thin-slice blade that I would never use anything else. I can do a bushel of beans julienne-style in 35 minutes. However, not all food processors do as good a job. If I had to buy a **bean slicer**, I would purchase the little handheld Krisk that sells for around $6. It is slow, but it does the best job.

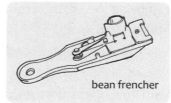

bean frencher

Several **apple peelers** are on the market; some work better than others. Ask for a demonstration before you purchase one. I consider my apple peeler a nice extra, not a necessary piece of equipment. Unless you put up bushels of sliced apples, you will not find much use for a peeler.

If you are planning to make jams and jellies, or to can fruit juices, a **thermometer** is very useful. Although plenty of tests can determine when jelly has gelled, nothing is as reliable as a good thermometer.

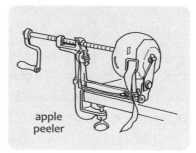

apple
peeler

Freezing Aids

In my opinion, boilable bags and automatic sealers are one of the most convenient and versatile food freezing aids to come along. As you will see in chapter 4, you can save a lot of time when freezing vegetables by packing the prepared produce in boilable bags, then blanching, cooling, and freezing — right in the bags. Then, when it comes time to cook the vegetables, you can even reheat them in the bag (although some are best steamed or stir-fried). These bags can also be used for freezing and reheating freshly made casseroles, soups, and stews in single-size portions.

Boilable bags have been reviewed by the FDA and found to be completely safe for processing and cooking foods. (If you have trouble finding them, try one of the mail-order companies that specialize in products for gardeners listed in the appendix). They are made of heavy-duty, food-safe plastic.

Automatic sealers work by sealing the top of the bag on a small, heated strip inside the appliance. Some sealers are designed to use continuous rolls so that you can custom-cut the size bag you need. Other models will seal different foods in separate sections of the same bag, allowing you to put together an entire meal at a time.

Still, you can achieve good results even without an automatic sealer by filling a boilable bag and placing it on a heavy bath towel, then covering the bag with a damp cloth and sealing the top with an electric iron set on low. The electric iron isn't as convenient as the automatic bag sealer, but trying the process with an iron will let you know whether you want to invest in the equipment.

Another particularly popular food preserving aid these days is the vacuum packaging machine. This type of sealer is more expensive but does a very good job of removing air from the package and thus reducing the chance of oxidation, which can lower the quality of the food. Vacuum-packed foods also take less room in the freezer. However, vacuum packed bags are generally not boilable, so you will need to blanch vegetables before packaging them. If you choose this option, keep in mind that while vacuum-packaging inhibits oxidation, it can increase the risk of other (often nonodorous) bacteria, making it all the more important to process your food properly before packaging.

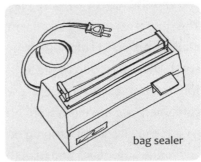

bag sealer

Blanchers, Preserving Kettles, and Canners

The pots in which you blanch vegetables, cook down relishes and jams, and process canned foods are necessary pieces of equipment. But before you buy anything new, take an inventory of what you have in your kitchen.

The traditional way of preparing vegetables for the freezer is to blanch the vegetables in boiling water to cover, cool them, drain, then bag. It is not the fastest way — using the boilable bag method is, as we will see in chapter 3.

One **blancher** on the market is so handy I find many uses for it, even though I blanch most of my vegetables in the microwave. The 5-in-1 Pot Steam Blancher is a versatile little kettle made up of a 7-quart deep pan, a deep steam basket, a smaller colander-type of basket, a flat perforated container that holds about 2 cups, and a cover. It can be used for cooking and steam-blanching (three layers at a time), and the colander can be used for straining. It's the handiest pot in my kitchen and sells for about $30.

For blanching vegetables in a microwave, 1 pound at a time, you will need a 2-quart, microwave-safe container.

If your microwave container does not have a lid, you will have to cover the container with microwave-safe plastic wrap. The microwave-safe plastic wraps that contain polyvinyl chloride form the best seals. Use a big enough piece to allow for steam to collect inside the wrap. To safely remove the wrap from hot food, pierce the plastic with the tip of a knife to release the steam and peel the plastic up and away from the container.

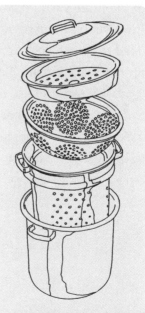

5-in-1 steam blancher

A **heavy-bottomed, large-capacity pot** is needed for making jams, jellies, and pickles, and for cooking down purées to make fruit leathers. It should be made of a nonreactive metal — that is, stainless steel, enamel-clad cast iron, anodized aluminum, or most nonstick finishes. These materials will not be affected by the acid in citrus juice, vinegar, fruit, or tomatoes. Pots made of unlined aluminum, copper, or cast iron may react with acidic foods to produce an off flavor or to discolor the food. The heavy bottom is necessary to disperse the heat evenly and prevent scorching, which is particularly important when you are making jams and chutneys.

Boiling-water-bath canners can be used to process acid foods only. Low-acid vegetables, meats, seafood, and mixes should never be canned in one (or without a properly researched pressure canning process). Boiling-water-bath canners come in two sizes — the smaller one can process up to 7 quarts at a time, and the larger size can process 9 quarts. They can be made of stainless steel, aluminum, or porcelain-on-steel — the latter being the least expensive, selling for $15 to $25. Any large kettle can be used in place of this type of canner as long as it is deep enough to accommodate quart size canning jars as well as a rack to set them on, plus 4 inches. It should have a cover in order to keep up a good rolling boil throughout the canning process.

Miscellaneous Items You Probably Already Own

A set of glass measuring cups is useful for measuring and pouring hot jellies, thin sauces, sugar syrups, and brines. They have the advantage of being safe for the microwave. Likewise, it's handy to have more than one set of measuring spoons, particularly when you are measuring a lot of different ingredients for pickles and relishes.

Final Thoughts

If you were to ask me what equipment I considered indispensable in my harvest kitchen, I would answer without hesitation: my freezer, dishwasher, food processor, hand-cranked strainer, and blender. I purchased each of these appliances as soon as they became available for home use, and I can assure you that over the years, they have paid for themselves many times over.

A dishwasher is one of the best time-saving appliances that you can invest in. It will wash several batches of canning or freezing jars at once and keep them hot until needed. Also, dishwashers are helpful with the everyday cleanup chores that need to be done during all seasons.

A dehydrator for less than $100 is a good alternative to a freezer, but a freezer allows you to save time and produce a more palatable end product.

Many more gadgets and appliances are available on the market. Most are unnecessary, but occasionally, something good comes along. If you find an item that looks like it might work for you, and you can afford it, give it a try. After all, it's the fun of experimenting that takes our daily lives out of the ordinary.

tips ❖ If you cannot afford some of the larger pieces of food processing equipment, you might consider getting together with two or three friends and sharing the cost. This arrangement will mean that you must either stagger harvest dates or plan to process foods together in sort of a mini-cooperative.

❖ As you buy new kitchen appliances, put the directions for assembly and use, parts order slips, and warranties in a drawer; or make up a loose-leaf binder with them, and put it with your cookbooks. This action will save time when using these appliances for the first few times, to say nothing of the aggravation that comes from looking for these papers when they are scattered all over, or when you need to have the appliance repaired.

CHAPTER 2

Tips, Hints, and Other Shortcuts

THE *BEST* WAY TO PRESERVE FRUITS and vegetables is to pick them at the peak of their maturity and get them from garden to freezer or dehydrator or canner immediately. However, given our busy daily schedules, this is *almost* impossible for most of us. I emphasize "almost" because, with proper advance planning, you can find the time to preserve everything your garden produces. "But," you say, "all the planning in the world won't prevent the green beans from ripening in the middle of the week when I have the least amount of time. Then what do I do?" The following pages contain all the time-saving tips I have gathered during my years of preserving fresh fruits and vegetables.

Ten Harvesting Tips

✸ **Timing planting.** If you stagger the planting dates of vegetables, they won't all be ready at the same time. This will make it easy to harvest and process small batches of vegetables frequently in short blocks of time.

✸ **Timing picking.** Vegetables picked late in the afternoon or early in the evening (with a few exceptions) will keep better. They have been manufacturing natural sugars and nutrients all day; once the sun goes down, they will use up part of these sugars and nutrients and are at their low ebb early in the morning.

✸ **Quality.** Pick only the best vegetables for storing. Use bruised or less perfect produce for daily meals.

✸ **Avoid bruising.** When picking produce, handle with care to prevent bruising.

✸ **Morning picking.** Berries keep better if they are picked early in the day.

✸ **Shallow containers.** When picking berries, collect the fruit in small containers to avoid packed and crushed fruit. As soon as each small container is filled, place it in the shade.

✸ **Short-term storage.** Store small amounts of fruits and vegetables in a refrigerator or ice chest. Place berries in colanders when refrigerating.

✸ **Short-term storage in large cans.** To make good containers for extra produce, punch drainage holes in large plastic or metal garbage cans. Put a layer of ice in the bottom, and cover with folded newspapers. Place the fresh fruit or vegetables in plastic bags on the newspapers, then place another layer of ice on the bags, and cover with more newspapers to keep in the cold. Set the can in a shady, protected spot. This will keep produce fresh for 2 to 3 days. Add fresh ice daily.

✸ **Short-term storage in appliances.** Fruits and vegetables, along with large ice packs or plastic jugs of ice wrapped in plastic bags to prevent leaking (condensation forms on the outside of jugs of ice), can be stored temporarily in your dishwasher, electric clothes dryer, or electric oven. (Do not use gas ovens with pilot lights.) Place a heavy towel in the bottom of the appliance; add the ice, then the fruits or vegetables. The insulation that prevents heat loss from these appliances will also keep in the cold. If you must store the produce for longer than 24 hours, change the ice. Return the melted ice packs or jugs to the freezer and refreeze for another time.

✳ **Washing.** Do not wash fruits and vegetables that will be stored before processing. Wash when you are ready to freeze, dry, or can.

Sixteen Preserving Tips

YOU WILL FIND MOST OF MY TIPS FOR SAVING TIME in chapters 3, 4, and 5 where I talk about specific ways of preserving food. Here are just a few reminders.

✳ **Tray-freezing vegetables.** If you find yourself faced with mounds of vegetables and not enough time to process the lot of them, try tray-freezing them. Wash and drain or dry the vegetables, and then dice or chop. (The smaller the pieces are, the faster they will freeze.) Spread the vegetables out on a few cookie sheets, place in the coolest part of your freezer, and allow to freeze. Once frozen, pour the vegetables into plastic bags. Chopped fresh vegetables can be frozen without blanching to be used within 2 months, if they are to be used in relishes or sauces. The crisp texture of the relish will suffer a little loss, but few people will notice it. Make sure when defrosting that all the juices are collected in a bowl and used in the recipe as part of the liquid.

✳ **Tray-freezing berries.** The fastest way to preserve berries is to wash them in cold water, lift the berries from the water, place in a colander, and drain well. Tray-freeze without sugar. When frozen solid, pack loosely in freezer bags. These berries can be used as you would use fresh berries for jams, jellies, pies, puddings, and sauces.

✸ **Applesauce.** The fastest and easiest method of making applesauce is with a hand-cranked strainer. Apples need not be peeled or
cored, just cooked until soft and puréed in the strainer. Applesauce
can be frozen or canned.

✸ **Quality fruit.** Use only firm, unblemished fruit to freeze for pies,
fruit compotes, and shortcakes. Soft, overripe fruit will turn to mush
when defrosted.

✸ **Purées.** Overripe, unblemished fruits can be frozen sliced or
whole (if small) to make quick purées when defrosted. Pop the
defrosted fruits into a blender or food processor to make a smooth
purée in an instant. Strain only if a very smooth purée is desired.

✸ **Juice into jelly.** Another way to deal with mounds of fruits that
have ripened all at once is to freeze or can them as juices to be made
into jellies when you have the time.

✸ **Pumpkins and squash.** Even if you don't have a proper root cellar, you can store pumpkins and winter squash until late in the fall or
winter when you have more time for processing. Keep the squash
and pumpkins on a closet floor after curing, and they will keep well
for 2 to 3 months in these dark, cooler places.

✸ **Tree fruits.** Apples, peaches, and pears should be sliced into a
bowl of water containing lemon juice or ascorbic acid to prevent
darkening. When all the fruit is prepared, drain well, and tray-freeze
or can in syrup.

✸ **Preparing syrups for fruits.** Prepare syrup for syrup-packed frozen fruits and berries ahead of time when you have a few extra
minutes; it will save time when preserving the fruits.

✸ **Microwaving syrups.** Sugar syrups can be made in glass measuring
cups and heated in the microwave. Heat until the mixture boils, stirring once halfway through the cooking time. Remove and stir to make
sure the sugar has completely dissolved. You can hold the syrup for up
to 60 minutes with the microwave set on WARM (10% power).

* **Clearest jellies.** To obtain a very clear jelly, strain fruit in muslin bags overnight. Do not press the fruit in the bag. If juice remains in the fruit, press the fruit in another bowl to extract the extra juice. Use this second extraction for another batch of less clear jelly.

* **Avoid crystallization.** To eliminate the problem of sugar crystals in freezer jams and jellies, measure the prepared fruit into a food processor, add sugar, and blend for 30 seconds. Let the fruit stand in the food processor for the length of time specified in the recipe, add the pectin mixture, and blend again for 30 seconds. While this technique is effective for freezer jams and jellies, it is not recommended for cooked or canned jams because air incorporated during the blending process can prove problematic.

* **Firm strawberries.** To keep strawberries from absorbing large quantities of water, do not hull them before washing.

* **Seedless jams.** To remove seeds from berries and grapes for jams and conserves, purée in the Squeezo strainer with the berry strainer.

* **Defrosting berries.** The best way to defrost tray-frozen berries is to place them in a bowl and cover with whatever sweetener you will be using in your recipe; do not stir. Cover the bowl tightly to prevent exposure to air (the berries will retain better color, texture, and flavor) and keep it in the refrigerator until the fruit thaws.

* **Fruit pies and muffins.** To make pies or muffins using tray-frozen fruits or berries, do not defrost before adding to the piecrust or batter. Add a few extra minutes to the baking time for muffins and 15 to 20 minutes for pies. This extra time may necessitate covering the edges of the piecrust with foil for the first part of the baking time to prevent overbaked edges. Increase the amount of thickening for berry pies by half again as much. For example, if your recipe calls for 2 tablespoons of quick-cooking tapioca, use 3 tablespoons.

Eight Tips for Setting Up an Efficient Work Flow

ARRANGE YOUR KITCHEN FOR GREATER EFFICIENCY prior to the harvest season. Having a place for everything will save time, work, and frustration. Here are some suggestions.

※ **Stow seasonal items.** Pack away seasonal dishes and entertainment items that take up a lot of shelf or cupboard space to free kitchen space for better harvest time use. Plastic laundry baskets make good storage containers for out-of-season items because they can be labeled and stacked in a small area.

※ **Eat elsewhere.** If possible, set up a dining area for your family in a room other than your kitchen to allow you to keep your work area set up at all times during the peak of the harvest season.

※ **Use a picnic table.** If possible, bring a picnic table into your kitchen for a large work area. The tops of most of these tables are just the right thickness for clamping on food processing equipment. I have found that if you are a short person, it is less tiring to use equipment with a crank handle on these tables because they are slightly lower than the average counter.

※ **Shoe-bag holder.** Hook a shoe bag with deep pockets to the inside of a door off your kitchen or pantry to hold small kitchen tools.

※ **Herb-and-spice assortment.** Make sure you have plenty of fresh herbs and spices. Take the time to mark the date on new containers as you open them. Once opened, herbs and ground spices should be used within 6 months, and whole spices within 1 year. After that they should be discarded because they lose flavor.

※ **Spice storage.** Use the inside doors on kitchen cupboards to mount spice racks. They won't collect dust and grease and will keep spices and herbs visible and quickly accessible. Line up spices and herbs in alphabetical order.

* **Closet storage spaces.** Closets are usually dark and cooler than the rest of the house, so they make good food storage spaces. Make use of the backs of closet doors. Inexpensive racks are available that will hold as many as 50 to 55 quart jars. Steel canning shelves that will fit in large closets will hold up to 220 quart jars.
* **Lazy Susan.** To fill jam and jelly jars quickly and easily, set the jars on a lazy Susan next to your preserve kettle. Rotate the lazy Susan as you fill the jars.

Twenty Ways to Make Life Easier During the Harvest

IF GARDENING AND FOOD PRESERVATION are to be an important part of your life, take steps to fit them smoothly into your schedule. Many things can be done year-round to make the harvest season less frantic and tiring. These shortcuts can be incorporated into your regular work schedule, and you won't even miss the few extra minutes that most of these tasks take.

* **Planning calendar.** Start by obtaining a calendar with large empty squares. Plan your year-round activities dealing with food preservation, and mark the times for these activities on this calendar. Variations or cancellations will occur, but important projects won't be forgotten and will be done on time.

FALL THROUGH LATE WINTER

* **Buying equipment.** Shop for food preservation equipment in the fall to save time and money. This equipment usually goes on sale right after the harvest season.
* **Involve the whole family.** Take the time to teach each member of the family how to do simple jobs: set the table, clear the dishes after meals, run the dishwasher, do the laundry, make beds, dust, vacuum,

and so on. Teach others in the family to do the grocery shopping by taking them with you a few times to learn the layout of the store, understand unit pricing, and be ready to share shopping chores at the busiest harvest time.

Stock up on stock. Make soup stocks to store in the freezer for quick, fresh vegetable soups in the summer. This idea is especially good if you heat with wood or coal stoves; you can use the energy for cooking that you are already using to heat your home.

Plan crops for use. Plan the types of foods you want to preserve before you plant your garden. For instance, if you want to can or freeze large quantities of tomato juice, any good tomato will do. On the other hand, if you plan to make ketchup, spaghetti sauce, or chili sauce, Italian plum tomatoes are the type you should plant. Try a few plants of Burpee's Longkeeper. These tomatoes can be harvested and left on a shelf to ripen well into the winter without spoiling.

Timed planting. Plan your vegetable garden, setting down approximate planting dates for various vegetables to stagger the harvest. This will prevent the problems that arise when everything is ready at the same time.

Research harvest recipes. Go through your recipe files and cookbooks to find your favorite summertime recipes as well as new ones you'd like to try, especially those using vegetables that you will be preserving. Aim for easy, quick-to-prepare dishes. Put these recipes in a special file.

Collect preserving recipes. Collect recipes for sauces, jams, jellies, preserves, pickles, and relishes (see recipe section for more). Put these recipes together in your special summertime file or create a new one for them.

Stock up on supplies. Once you have decided which recipes you would like to try, calculate how much sugar, pickling salt, spices, vinegar, and freezer bags you will need, and buy a little each time you shop. This will save extra shopping trips at your busiest time and spread the cost of the extras over a longer period of time.

* **Jar storage.** Clear at least one large shelf in a clean, enclosed area (kitchen cupboard, nearby closet, or pantry) to store canning jars that can be washed ahead of time.

EARLY SPRING THROUGH EARLY SUMMER

* **Meals ahead.** As winter slips into early spring, prepare extra meals to tuck away in the freezer for harvest day dinners that are fairly effortless to put on the table.

* **Sewing for harvest time.** Make little muslin herb and spice bags, food straining bags, heavy potholders, and cover-all aprons. Aprons save on laundry and can be made easily from old shirts. Just remove the collars and sleeves and finish off the rough edges with binding tape. For the little ones, make large bibs out of old flannel-backed plastic tablecloths and some bias tape.

* **Recycled strainers.** Old stockings and panty hose make handy food strainers. Cut the crotch and feet out of clean, old panty hose, tie or sew one end of the leg, and use them for extra straining bags.

* **Examine canning jars.** Check your canning jars for nicks and cracks; discard those unsafe for food storage.

* **Locate markets.** To save time in late summer, locate farmers' markets or truck gardens in your area in the late spring or early summer. Vegetables and fruits from these sources can supplement your own garden produce.

* **Spring cleaning.** As your root cellar empties in the spring, clean the shelves well to avoid insect and bacteria problems during the warmer months.

* **Defrost the freezer.** Defrost and clean your freezer late in the spring. (Use a hair dryer to hasten the defrosting if necessary.) Remove all frozen foods from plastic containers and refreeze the food in marked plastic bags. The foods will come out of the plastic containers easily if you run a little hot water over the bottom and sides. Wash containers in warm, sudsy water containing baking soda to get rid of unwanted odors. Throw away all foods that are

past their prime, or use them as soon as possible in soups, stews, or casseroles. Those that must be discarded should go out to the compost pile.

❋ **Prepare temporary cold storage.** Scrub out any extra garbage cans you have, or buy a new one. In the height of the harvest season, you can fill these cans with ice and produce to keep your vegetables fresh and chilled.

❋ **Cut freezer costs.** To save on the cost of running your freezer, fill it with ice packs (see page 31) or milk cartons of water as it empties. A full freezer costs less to run, and the ice will come in handy to cool blanched vegetables.

❋ **Preseason workshops.** Get together with a group of friends and encourage local stores and Cooperative Extension Services to give food preservation classes in the late spring prior to the harvest season, rather than during harvest season when you are too busy to attend.

CHAPTER 3

Basic Techniques for Preserving Food

THE EASIEST, FASTEST, OLDEST METHOD of food preservation is root cellaring, or cold storage. However, many fruits and vegetables do not adapt well to cold storage, many homes do not have root cellars, and root cellars are best suited for climates where average winter temperatures are 30°F or lower.

Freezing is also fast and easy, but not all produce freezes well and many people don't own large freezers.

Dehydrating, or drying, foods is an ancient preservation method that comes with its own pros and cons. It requires little in the way of preparation, compared to freezing and canning. And although the process is time-consuming, you are free to be elsewhere while the dehydrator, the oven, or the sun does the work. Dried foods also are easy to store and have a long shelf life.

DRYING DOES INTENSIFY THE FLAVORS OF FOODS, which can be good or bad, depending on your point of view. Not all foods are good candidates for drying.

Canning is probably the most time-consuming method of food preservation, but sometimes it results in the very best product. So, instead of ignoring canning altogether, I will show you ways of saving time when doing it — so that you can have the very best home-preserved foods.

The key to saving time when you process food is to be very organized. Make sure your equipment is ready and your tasks are sorted out. Ideally, you can share these tasks with other members of the family. Here is a step-by-step method for each food preservation technique. Take the time to study the methods carefully; then turn to the sections on the individual vegetables and fruits for more details, and follow those brief steps to process the fruits and vegetables you have on hand with the method that suits you best.

Root Cellaring (or Cold Storage)

IF YOU ARE ONE OF THE LUCKY PEOPLE who have a storage area that will keep foods cool without freezing them (generally 32°F to 40°F), you can store some fruits (apples, grapefruit, grapes, and pears) and vegetables (shell beans, beets, cabbages, carrots, cauliflower, celery, kohlrabi, onions, peppers, potatoes, pumpkins, winter squash, and green tomatoes) without processing. Or you can temporarily store these vegetables until the rush of the harvest season and the winter holidays is over. With more space in your freezer and many canning jars emptied, you can process apples, beets, carrots, cauliflower, pumpkins, and tomatoes at your leisure.

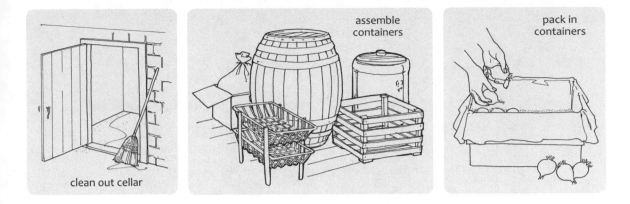

clean out cellar

assemble containers

pack in containers

STORING IN A ROOT CELLAR: Six Easy Steps

❶ Clean your root cellar or storage area once a year, just before the harvest season. Sweep out the area, scrub all your containers, and leave the area open to air for a few days.

❷ Assemble your containers. Since different fruits and vegetables have different storage requirements — some like it cool and dry, some like it cool and moist — you will need to provide different conditions. Onions, pumpkins, and squash need dry conditions with plenty of air circulation. Root vegetables like it moist; store them in sturdy boxes, barrels, large plastic bags, or crocks. Packing fruits and vegetables in layers of dried leaves, straw, or crumpled newspapers will help absorb excess odors.

❸ Harvest the best produce. Remove any injured or overripe produce and use immediately.

❹ Prepare each vegetable as needed. For winter squash and pumpkins, this means leaving them to dry in the sun. Onions should be dried before storing. Read the sections on individual vegetables for specifics.

❺ Pack the unwashed fruits and vegetables in suitable containers.

❻ Check your stored foods from time to time. Remove any that are beginning to soften or show signs of spoiling. If possible, use immediately or freeze or can.

Basic Techniques for Preserving Food

27

Freezing

FREEZING MAINTAINS THE NATURAL COLOR, fresh flavor, and high nutritive value of fresh foods. The objective is to bring foods to the frozen state quickly. When properly done, fruits and vegetables are more like fresh than when preserved by any other method. Best of all, freezing is fast and easy.

I had been freezing garden surpluses for years when I began experimenting with the process. I discovered that the old standard method of washing and preparing the vegetables, then blanching, cooling, drying, packing, and freezing them was not always the fastest, easiest way to produce the best finished product. Many vegetables can be frozen without blanching (although their shelf lives in the freezer will be shorter), and greens can be stir-fried instead of blanched for a better product. I'll go over each method step by step, but first, a few words about organizing your work and getting your packaging materials ready.

> tip ❋ To prevent injury when slicing vegetables with a manually operated rotary slicer, blade slicer, or slaw slicer, wear a clean cotton garden glove on the hand that is apt to come in contact with the slicing blade.

PACKAGING FROZEN FOODS

Proper packaging is absolutely necessary to prevent freezer burn, oxidation, and formation of large ice crystals.

For freezing most of the vegetables in this book, I strongly recommend using *boilable bags.* These heavy-duty freezer bags allow you to blanch, cool, freeze, then cook your vegetables right in the bag. They are sealed with an automatic sealer or your own electric flat iron. It is very important that you use bags the manufacturer specifies as boilable since many plastic food storage bags are not suitable for heating.

Other freezer packaging materials you can use are freezer paper, heavy foil, widemouthed freezer jars with straight sides (for easy removal of frozen foods), rigid plastic containers, and plastic freezer bags. Square freezer jars or rigid containers make better use of freezer space than round ones. If you don't use boilable bags, use only heavy-duty plastic bags that are labeled "food safe."

It is important to remove as much air as possible from packages of food before freezing. Excess air in the packages causes oxidation, which lowers the quality of the food, and vacuum-packed bags take up less freezer space.

If you plan to use a vacuum packaging machine, please review the information on freezing aids in chapter 1, and be sure to follow the manufacturer's directions.

Accessories on the market remove air from plastic bags, but you can effectively remove air without investing any money, by pressing it out with a pillow or your hand. This method works best with boilable bags.

1 Fill the boilable bag with vegetables and distribute the vegetables evenly in the bag.

2 With a small pillow or your hand, press down gently, but firmly, on the bag to expel all the air you can.

3 Hold the bag closed between your thumb and forefinger. Press the sealing bar down and hold a few seconds longer than recommended. Move the bag ½ inch and seal again.

| partially seal | remove the air | complete seal |

If you don't have an automatic bag sealer, use an electric flat iron, as follows:

1 Heat the iron on its cotton setting.

2 Place a filled bag on a heavy towel, and place a damp cotton cloth over the edge of the bag.

3 Partially seal the bag with an iron, leaving 1½ inches open.

4 Remove the air by pressing a small pillow or your hand on the bag, gently but firmly.

5 Finish sealing with the electric iron over the damp cotton cloth.

WASHING VEGETABLES AND FRUIT

Wash your vegetables and fruit in plenty of water. Use a medium-stiff-bristled brush or a plastic or nylon net scrubber that can get into crevices where the dirt is hardest to remove. Be especially thorough with root crops, since botulism bacteria may be in the soil and only thorough washing will remove them.

Always lift produce out of the water rather than letting the water drain off. Drain vegetables on a towel, patting as dry as possible.

REUSABLE ICE PACKS

It's worth investing in a box of quart-size boilable freezer bags to make ice packs for freezing. Use those bags, instead of cubes or chunks of ice, to quick-chill blanched food (see pages 36 to 39). When you are through freezing for the day, remove the bags from the water, wipe them dry with a towel, and return them to the freezer to refreeze. This saves the fuss of making ice cubes and the frustration of running out of ice in the middle of a large freezing project, and the bags of ice last much longer than either ice cubes or chunks of ice. Here's how you can make these ice packs.

1 Fill a boilable freezer bag three-quarters full of cold water.

2 Hold the bag over the edge of your shelf or counter.

3 Seal with electric sealer, or place the bag on a towel, cover with a damp cloth, and press with a hot iron. Freeze.

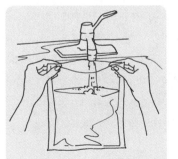

fill bag with water

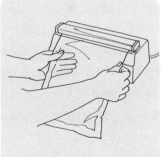

seal with electric sealer

UNBLANCHED FREEZING: FIVE QUICK STEPS

This is the fastest, easiest method of freezing. It was originally thought that this method was acceptable only for chopped onions, peppers, fresh herbs, or other vegetables that were to be stored for less than 1 month. But I have found that many unblanched, frozen vegetables can be stored for up to twice as long and still maintain good color, flavor, and texture. Try this method with onions, peppers, herbs, celery, corn in husks, cabbage, sugar snap peas, summer squash, young tender broccoli, and green beans. It is the preferred method to use with berries. It can also be used with super-quality fruits, especially ones you plan to use semi-thawed, or baked in a dessert such as a crisp or a crumble.

cooking tip ✿ Frozen, unblanched vegetables are best cooked by stir-frying. To do so, melt 1 teaspoon of butter per serving in a heavy, preheated skillet. When the butter has melted, add the frozen vegetables and stir and toss the vegetables over high heat to the desired degree of tenderness. Cook until all moisture is evaporated. If more moisture is needed to cook to desired stage of doneness, add water, 1 tablespoon at a time.

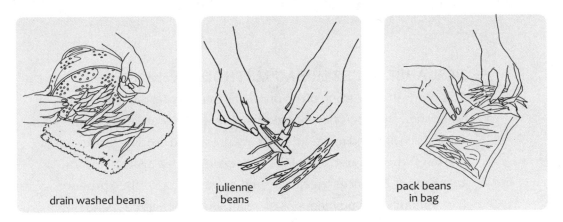

drain washed beans

julienne beans

pack beans in bag

1 Make sure your work area and all equipment are spotlessly clean. Assemble your equipment and set your tools where they will be most useful. You will need a scrubbing brush, towels, freezer bags, a small pillow (optional), and a labeling pen and tape.

2 Select vegetables that are slightly immature. Wash the vegetables and drain on towels.

3 Prepare the vegetables: slice, dice, chop, julienne, or leave whole. Leave berries whole; peel and slice or chop other fruit.

4 Pack in freezer bags, expelling as much air as possible. Label with name of product and date.

5 Freeze in a single layer in the coldest part of the freezer.

Vegetables and fruits frozen this way should be used within 6 to 8 weeks. The best methods of cooking vegetables frozen in this manner are stir-frying and steaming.

Basic
Techniques
for
Preserving
Food

tip ❖ The more accessible the proper tools for food processing are, the faster, easier, and more enjoyable the job will be. After using large appliances, such as food processors, I always wash and set them back up again. I cover my strainer with a plastic bag to prevent dirt and bacteria from collecting in the open funnel top.

BOILABLE FREEZER BAG METHOD: Twelve Steps

This method of freezing often produces the best-tasting vegetables. Since the vegetables never come in contact with water, all color, flavor, texture, and most nutrients are preserved. Adding butter to the bag, when desired, coats the vegetables with a protective film that further enhances the quality and flavor of the finished product. Experiment with combinations of vegetables, such as peas and tiny onions, or peas and carrots. Sliced, diced, or julienne vegetables work best. Whole carrots and beets do not freeze well by this method. Strong-flavored vegetables, such as broccoli, cauliflower, cabbage, and turnips, should not be frozen by this method.

Time is saved with this method because bags of food can be blanched in multiples; cooling requires no special timing or handling (allowing you to continue packing); and since all vegetables are processed within the package, pans need only to be rinsed and dried, making cleanup a snap.

I tested this method against the standard freezing method with green beans. After the initial washing and trimming (time for both was the same), I timed the balance of the freezing procedure. I was able to pack, blanch, and cool a half-bushel of green beans by the boilable freezer bag method in 29 minutes, versus 1 hour and 25 minutes for the standard method. Try it yourself!

The real challenge with this method is locating a bag sealer and suitable freezer bags. If you can't find a source locally, check the mail-order listings on page 224.

1 Make sure your work area and all equipment are spotlessly clean. Assemble your equipment and set your tools where they will be most useful. You will need a scrub brush, towels, a chopping board, knives, a food processor, a widemouthed funnel or large spoon, freezer bags, a small pillow (optional), a bag sealer or electric flat iron, an indelible marking pen and freezer tape, a large roaster half-filled with water for blanching, a large kettle for cooling, ice packs, cubes, or chunks of ice, tongs, potholders, and a timer.

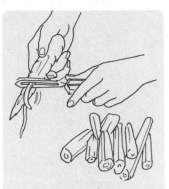

pare produce

· · · · · · · · · · ·

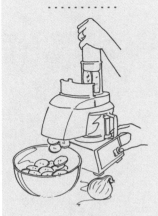

slice produce

expel air from bag

· · · · · · · · · · ·

seal with electric sealer

2 Select young, fresh vegetables that are just table-ready or slightly immature. Wash well; drain on towels.

3 Begin heating water in the roaster for blanching.

4 Prepare vegetables as desired: slice, dice, chop, julienne, or leave whole (except for large, dense vegetables, such as carrots and beets).

5 Plug in the bag sealer or iron. Fill four boilable bags with vegetables in meal-size portions, making sure that when the vegetables are distributed, the package is no thicker than 1 inch. Add butter and seasonings if desired. Use as much as you would use if cooking for a meal.

6 Expel as much air as possible and seal with the automatic bag sealer. Or place the bag on a towel, cover with a damp cloth, and seal with an electric iron. Label and date bag.

7 When four bags are packed, drop them into the boiling water and blanch with the pan covered. (The bags will float on top of the water. This is all right, as long as each bag has one side in contact with the boiling water.) Check the timing (see chart on page 220) and set the timer. A rule of thumb is to blanch for double the length of time suggested for the standard blanching method. Use a slightly shorter time for tender young vegetables, and a slightly longer time for more mature ones. Start counting the time as soon as you replace the cover.

8 Fill the cooling kettle with cold water and ice packs (see page 31) or cubes or chunks of ice.

Continue packing while the first batch is blanching.

9 When the blanching time is up, remove the packages from the blanching kettle and place them in the ice water. Make sure the ice holds the bags down in the water, since air left in the bag tends to make the bags float. During the chilling time, occasionally knead the bags to move the cold into the center of the packages.

10 Add four more bags to the blancher and continue as before, until all the vegetables are blanched. Leave the processed bags in the ice until you are completely finished, unless you need the space for more vegetables.

When all the vegetables have been blanched, leave the bags in the ice water for an additional 10 minutes. While the bags are cooling, clean up your work area.

11 Remove the bags of vegetables from the water and dry with towels.

12 Freeze the vegetables in a single layer in the coldest part of the freezer. Remove the ice bags from the cooling kettle, pat dry, and return to the freezer.

Foods frozen this way can be cooked in the bag or removed and steamed or stir-fried for faster cooking.

drop bag into boiling water

prepare cooling kettle

chill bags in ice water

dry bags with towel

MICROWAVE BLANCHING METHOD FOR FREEZING:
Nine Steps

This method of freezing often produces great-tasting vegetables. Since the vegetables are not immersed in water, all color, flavor, texture, and most nutrients are preserved. Adding butter to the vegetables coats them with a protective film that further enhances the quality and flavor of the finished product. Experiment with combinations of vegetables, such as peas and tiny onions, or peas and carrots. Sliced, diced, or julienned vegetables work best. To promote even cooking, most vegetables require stirring halfway through the blanching process.

Please note: Microwave blanching for the freezer is not a tried-and-true method. Your local County Extension Service agent won't recommend it, as research has shown that all enzymes may not be destroyed by this method. This probably relates to the differing efficiencies of various microwave models, plus how evenly the vegetables were placed in the blanching container and whether or not the vegetables were stirred halfway through the blanching time. Note, too, that the individual blanching times per pound of vegetable are about the same as for blanching vegetables on top of the stove, plus you have to add stirring time. However, there is no time wasted while you wait for the water to return to a boil on top of the stove — and that is where the time-savings come in.

1 Make sure your work area and all equipment are spotlessly clean. Assemble your equipment and set your tools where they will be most useful. You will need a scrub brush, a colander, strainers, paring and chopping knives, a cutting board, a food processor (optional), measuring cups, tongs, towels, waxed-paper-lined cookie sheets, freezer containers or bags, freezer tape and an indelible marking pen, a large microwave-safe container with lid or microwave-safe plastic wrap, potholders, and a timer.

2 Select young, fresh vegetables that are just table-ready or slightly immature. Wash, and drain on absorbent towels.

3 Prepare the vegetables as desired: slice, dice, chop, julienne, or leave whole.

4 Clean the sink and fill with water and ice packs (see page 31) or cubes or chunks of ice.

5 Blanch the vegetables. Work in 3- to 4-cup batches (1 to 1½ pounds). Arrange the vegetables in a large, shallow microwave-safe container and add ¼ to ½ cup water. Cover with plastic wrap. Set the timer and blanch. Specific amounts for vegetables and water, as well as specific times, can be found for each vegetable on the chart found on page 221.

6 Cool the vegetables quickly in ice water. Cooling time is approximately the same as blanching.

7 Drain the vegetables thoroughly, removing as much water as possible by lifting them from the ice water onto towels and patting them dry with another towel. While one batch of vegetables is chilling, pack any previously drained batches, and blanch another.

8 Place cooled, drained vegetables on waxed-paper-lined cookie sheets and freeze until solid. Then package loosely in plastic bags that have been labeled with the date and product. Be sure to remove as much air as possible. You can package these vegetables in large bags and remove just the number of servings needed at a time. You can also package the vegetables in freezer containers.

9 Freeze vegetables in a single layer in the coldest part of the freezer. Clean up when all vegetables are in the freezer. Wipe ice packs dry and return to the freezer.

STANDARD FREEZING METHOD: Ten Steps

Pick up any book on food preservation written before the days of microwaves or boilable bags, or written without concern for saving time, and you will find this method. It works just fine and you get a very acceptable end product, but you will spend more time with it.

1 Make sure your work area and all equipment are spotlessly clean. Assemble your equipment and set your tools where they will be most useful. You will need a scrub brush, a colander, strainers, paring and chopping knives, a cutting board, food processing equipment (optional), measuring cups, tongs, towels, waxed-paper-lined cookie sheets, freezer containers or bags, freezer tape and an indelible marking pen, a blanching kettle half-filled with water, potholders, and a timer.

2 Select young fresh vegetables that are just table-ready or slightly immature. Wash and drain on towels.

3 Begin heating water in the blanching kettle.

4 Prepare the vegetables as desired: slice, dice, chop, julienne, or leave whole.

5 Clean the sink and fill with water and ice packs (see page 31) or cubes or chunks of ice.

6 Blanch the vegetables. If you have a boiling-water blancher, immerse the vegetables in boiling water, 1 pound at a time. Start counting as soon as the water returns to a boil, and blanch as long

Basic
Techniques
for
Preserving
Food

39

as the chart on page 220 indicates. If it takes longer than 2 minutes for the water to return to a boil, blanch fewer vegetables at a time.

If you have a steam blancher, blanch 1 pound of vegetables (arranged in a single layer) at a time in a steam basket or blancher suspended over boiling water. Steam the vegetables for half again as long as you would if you were blanching in boiling water. Start counting time as soon as you cover the pan. You can stack three blanchers to process up to 2½ pounds of vegetables at a time. Add 2 minutes to the blanching times, and begin counting time as soon as the pan is covered. It is a good idea to put the larger pieces of vegetables on the bottom and the smaller pieces at the top.

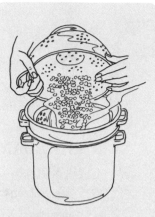

blanch the produce

7 Cool the vegetables quickly in ice water. Cooling time is approximately the same as blanching. Do not immerse the blanching utensil in the ice water — this will warm the water unnecessarily, requiring more ice or a longer cooling time; and when you return the blancher to the boiling water, it will require more time and energy to return the blancher to the boiling point.

cool in ice water

8 Drain the vegetables thoroughly, removing as much water as possible by lifting them from the ice water onto towels and patting them dry with another towel. While one batch of vegetables is chilling, pack any previously drained batches, and blanch another.

drain produce on towel

freeze on cookie sheet ⋮ fill meal-size bags

9 Line cookie sheets with waxed paper, place cooled, drained vegetables on sheets, and freeze until solid. Then package loosely in plastic bags that have been labeled with the date and product. Be sure to remove as much air as possible. You can package these vegetables in large bags and remove just the number of servings needed at a time. You can also package the vegetables in freezer containers.

10 Freeze vegetables in a single layer in the coldest part of the freezer. Clean up when all vegetables are in the freezer. Wipe ice packs dry and return to the freezer.

Drying

DRYING FOODS IS A NATURAL ALTERNATIVE for people with limited time and limited space for storing frozen or canned foods. Compared with canning, the process is much less complicated — and the only special equipment is a dehydrator, though it is possible to dry without one. Compared to freezing, it is less expensive and worry-free; power failures represent no threat to dried foods. Many foods can be dried, but I will focus on those that are most popularly dried: fruits and a few vegetables, including mushrooms, and herbs.

TO PRETREAT OR NOT TO PRETREAT

Drying foods, like freezing, does not stop the enzymatic action that causes fruit to mature and eventually decay; it only slows it down. Some foods keep well without pretreatment, but others will continue to deteriorate in color, flavor, texture, and nutrients for months after they have dried unless they are treated. Pretreatment can mean blanching, as you would do before freezing vegetables, or dipping the food in ascorbic acid, fruit juice, or a commercial preparation that contains ascorbic acid or sodium sulfite. Specific pretreatment recommendations are found with each vegetable and fruit listing in chapters 4 and 5.

Blanching. If you have a boiling-water blancher, immerse the vegetables in boiling water, 1 pound at a time. Start counting as soon as the water returns to a boil, and blanch as long as the chart on page 220 indicates. If it takes longer than 2 minutes for the water to return to a boil, blanch fewer vegetables at a time.

If you have a steam blancher, blanch 1 pound of vegetables (arranged in a single layer) at a time in a steam basket or blancher suspended over boiling water. Steam the vegetables for half again as long as you would if you were blanching in boiling water. Start counting time as soon as you cover the pan. You can stack three blanchers to process up to 2½ pounds of vegetables at a time. Add 2 minutes to the blanching times, and begin counting time as soon as the pan is covered. It is a good idea to put the larger pieces of vegetables on the bottom and the smaller pieces at the top.

If you have a microwave, arrange 3 to 4 cups of vegetables in a container and add ¼ to ½ cup water. Set the timer and blanch.

Specific amounts for vegetables and water, as well as specific times, can be found for each vegetable on the chart on page 221.

Cool the vegetables quickly in ice water. Cooling time is approximately the same as blanching. Drain the vegetables thoroughly, removing as much water as possible by lifting them from the ice water onto towels and patting them dry with another towel.

Ascorbic Acid Dip. Ascorbic acid is a form of vitamin C. Dissolve 2 tablespoons of ascorbic acid crystals, 2 tablespoons of ascorbic acid powder, or five crushed 1-gram vitamin C tablets in 1 quart of lukewarm water. Slice or chop fruits directly into the solution. When 1 or 2 cups of fruit have accumulated in the solution, give it a stir and remove the fruit with a slotted spoon. Drain well before loading drying trays.

Fruit Juice Dip. Dip peaches, apples, or banana slices into 1 quart undiluted pineapple juice or 1 quart lukewarm water into which ¼ cup lemon juice has been stirred. Let fruits remain in the dip for no more than 5 to 10 minutes. Drain well before drying.

TESTING DRIED FOODS

Before dried foods are stored, they should be tested to be sure enough moisture has been removed. If the foods have not been adequately dried, it is possible for mold and bacteria to grow and cause decay. Well-dried foods will vary from a moisture content of 5 percent for leafy vegetables, such as spinach, to 25 percent for juicy acid fruits, such as apricots. You can judge the percent of moisture by weighing the food before and after drying. One pound of fresh tomatoes will weigh 4 ounces when properly dried to a moisture level of 25 percent.

All dried foods should be cooled before testing for drying because warm foods feel more moist than when they have cooled. In general, dried foods feel dry when they are squeezed.

Root vegetables, squash, and pumpkin are dry when they are tough and leathery, still pliable, but with no moisture in the center. Celery should be hard and brittle. To test, cut through the center with a knife or take a bite of it.

Green beans should be dark green and leathery. Greens, such as spinach, should be brittle enough to crumble in the hands. Corn, peas, and dry beans should be dry enough to shatter or split in half when tapped with a hammer.

Fruits are dry when leathery enough that several pieces will spring back without sticking together after being squeezed. Fruits such as peaches, pears, apples, and plums should remain pliable. Berries, rhubarb, and lemon or orange peel should be crisp and brittle. Banana slices may be crisp or slightly pliable, depending on the thickness of the slices and the method of pretreatment.

Fruit leathers are still slightly sticky to the touch when they are dried, but will pull away from the plastic wrap easily. For long-term storage, dry leathers until they are no longer sticky.

Herb leaves are dry enough for storage when they are so brittle they will crumble easily in your hands.

tip ❖ Leathers have almost as many names as they have uses. The first settlers in the Old West made leathers to preserve the goodness of fruits and vegetables that would otherwise have gone to waste. They called them "papers" because of their paper-thinness, or "fruit leathers" because of their pliable, leathery texture. Today they may be called fruit rolls or fruit taffy because of their delicious, candylike taste.

STORING DRIED FOODS

Dried foods should be stored in small batches that are either vacuum-packed or sealed in airtight, insect-proof containers — glass or plastic jars or plastic freezer bags (avoid lightweight plastic, which can be slightly porous).

After the dried food has cooled, place it in a storage container and seal tightly. Don't delay this step, or the dried produce will begin to accumulate moisture. Watch for signs of moisture inside the jars or bags. If moisture appears, either the food is not dry or the container was not properly sealed. If there are no signs of mold, return the food to the dehydrator for further drying. Moldy foods should be thrown out.

Fruit leathers can be rolled in plastic wrap or waxed paper. Stand the rolls in a metal or glass container — clean, dry coffee cans work well — and seal with a tight-fitting lid.

Because their flavors are easily lost, herbs, herb mixtures, and herb teas are best stored separately in very small containers, such as clean, dry pill bottles or baby food jars. Be certain, though, that the bottles are odor-free. Herb leaves that are to be used within a few months usually are crumbled before storing, but for the best flavor retention in long-term storage, store the leaves intact and crumble just before using.

Keep containers in a cool, dark, dry place.

tips ✿ Dried foods can make lovely gifts. Fill small baby food jars with dried herbs or herb mixtures. Paste pretty labels on the jars and include a few recipes on decorative file cards. Or package a mixed variety of fruit leather strips in plastic wrap and tie with a big ribbon.

✿ There will be times when the weather is humid, or your dehydrator is overloaded, or it just isn't convenient to dry foods at harvest time. Apples, pears, onions, celery, squash, pumpkins, and carrots can be stored in a cool, dry storage room for a few weeks, until you are ready to dry them. Green peppers, corn, peaches, and strawberries can be stored in the freezer until a more convenient time. Blanch corn and peaches as you would for freezer storage, but the other fruit and vegetables need no pretreatment. For fruit leathers, purée the fruit in a blender, pour into a container, and freeze. When you are ready to make the leathers, just thaw and spread the purée on drying trays.

DRYING FOODS IN A DEHYDRATOR: Seven Steps

You will get the most consistent results with a dehydrator. And, dehydrator drying is so trouble-free you can leave the dehydrator operating overnight or while you're away from home. Consider loading the dehydrator in the morning before you leave for work and letting it run all day. If a dryer load is almost dry at bedtime, just reduce the heat to 105°F to 110°F and go to bed. By morning, the food will be ready to store.

1 Clean your work surface and assemble your tools. You will need knives, peelers, a cutting board, measuring cups and spoons and a bowl (if you are pretreating), a colander, and a towel. Dehydrators come complete with their own trays.

2 Select young, fresh vegetables that are just table-ready or slightly immature. Select firm, ripe fruit. Wash, and drain on towels.

3 Preheat the dehydrator to the desired temperature. Recommended temperatures are 115°F for uncooked fruits, 120°F for vegetables and some cooked fruits, and 110°F for leafy herbs.

4 Peel, slice, dice, chop, julienne, halve, or leave whole, depending on the recommendations for the specific fruit, vegetable, or herb. Pretreat or blanch according to the recommendations for each food.

5 Spread the prepared foods evenly over the dehydrator trays in thin layers. Different foods can be dried at the same time, but very moist foods should not be dried with almost-dry foods, nor should you combine foods with strong odors or flavors.

6 Dry according to the times specified for each food. Test for dryness according to the recommendations on pages 43 to 44. Rotate the trays front to back, side to side, and top to bottom at least once during the drying process. Also stir the food or turn it.

7 Package dried foods in airtight bottles, jars, or plastic bags. Store in a cool, dark place.

DRYING FOOD IN A CONVENTIONAL OVEN:
Seven Steps

Drying food in an oven is sometimes better than sun drying, because it is possible to have controlled, even temperatures, but it has the disadvantage of poor air circulation, and air movement is necessary for even drying. Air circulation can be improved by leaving the oven door ajar a few inches and placing an electric fan in front of the door, positioning it to blow away moist air as it accumulates.

Although commercial drying trays are available for use in an oven, homemade trays can be made of wooden frames and nylon screening. For air circulation, allow 1 inch of space on each side, 3 inches on top and bottom, and 2½ inches between trays.

❶ Clean your work surface and assemble your tools. You will need knives, peelers, a cutting board, measuring cups and spoons and a bowl (if you are pretreating), a colander, a towel, and storage containers. You will also need a thermometer that registers from 100°F to 150°F.

❷ Select young, fresh vegetables that are just table-ready or slightly immature. Select firm, ripe fruit. Wash, and drain on towels.

❸ Set a large, easily read thermometer on the top shelf of the oven and preheat to the desired temperature. Recommended temperatures are 115°F for uncooked fruits, 120°F for vegetables and some cooked fruits, and 110°F for leafy herbs.

❹ Peel, slice, dice, chop, julienne, halve, or leave whole, depending on the recommendations for the specific fruit, vegetable, or herb. Pretreat or blanch according to the recommendations for each food.

❺ Spread the prepared foods sparsely but evenly over the dehydrator trays in thin layers. Different foods can be dried at the same time, but very moist foods should not be dried with almost-dry foods, nor should you combine foods with strong odors or flavors.

6 Place the trays in the oven, leaving the door ajar. Set an electric fan in front of the door. Dry according to the directions for each food, stirring or turning the food occasionally and rotating the trays front to back, side to side, and top to bottom every 2 to 3 hours.

7 Package dried foods in airtight bottles, jars, or plastic bags. Store in a cool, dark place.

SUN-DRYING: Six Steps

If you are blessed with clean air, low humidity, and an abundance of hot, sunny days, sun-drying is the least expensive and simplest method of preserving fruits and herbs. But drying outdoors is unpredictable unless the temperatures are over 100°F and the relative humidity is low. If the temperature is too low, the humidity is too high, or both, spoilage will occur before drying is achieved. Because sun-drying is slower and food is exposed for a longer period of time, pretreating is more important than for drying in a dehydrator.

1 Clean your work surface and assemble your tools. You will need knives, peelers, a cutting board, measuring cups and spoons and a bowl (for pretreating), a colander, a towel, and storage containers. You will also need a cheesecloth for protecting food from insects and birds. Drying trays can be cookie sheets or homemade wooden trays, but drying is speeded if air is allowed to circulate freely, so trays made of fiberglass or stainless steel screening work best. Do not use galvanized screen, which will contaminate food.

2 Select firm, ripe fruit. Wash, and drain on towels.

3 Peel, slice, dice, chop, julienne, halve, or leave whole, depending on the recommendations for the specific fruit or herb. Pretreat or blanch according to the recommendations for each food.

4 Spread the prepared foods sparsely but evenly over the dehydrator trays in thin layers. Different foods can be dried at the same time. Cover with cheesecloth.

5 Place the trays in a well-ventilated spot in full sun. Every few hours, turn or stir the food. Take trays inside at night. (Do not include inside time when calculating drying time.)

6 Before storing, place food in the oven set at 125°F for 30 minutes to kill any insect eggs that may have been deposited on them, or place in the freezer for a day or two. Then package in airtight bottles, jars, or plastic bags. Store in a cool, dark place.

MAKING FRUIT LEATHERS: Four Steps

Any fruit (or vegetable) or combination of fruits can be made into leathers. Leathers are an excellent way to use slightly overripe fruits, which have more flavor than just-ripe fruit anyway. Leathers can be made from purées of raw or cooked fruits. You can add water or juice to the blender to get a mixture thin enough to pour. Figure that 2 cups of purée will fill a standard 10- by 15-inch rimmed baking sheet.

1 Strain cooked or thoroughly ripened raw fruit through a food mill or liquefy in a blender until you have a smooth purée. If needed, add juice or water to make the mixture thin enough to pour.

2 Line a drying tray with plastic wrap (or use the fruit leather sheet that came with your dehydrator). Spread the purée ½-inch thick on the drying tray.

Basic
Techniques
for
Preserving
Food

49

3 To dry in a dehydrator, set tray in dehydrator at 120°F for 6 to 8 hours, or until leather can be pulled easily from the plastic. Invert, pull off plastic, and continue drying for another 4 to 6 hours. To dry in a conventional oven, put tray in oven at 120°F for 6 to 8 hours or until leather can be pulled easily from the plastic. Invert, pull off plastic, and continue drying for another 6 to 8 hours. To dry in the sun, set tray outdoors for 1 day, or until leather can be pulled easily from plastic. Invert, pull off plastic, and dry for 1 more day. Bring trays inside at night.

4 To store, roll up in waxed paper or plastic wrap, close and twist ends and store in the refrigerator for up to 6 weeks.

Canning

DOES A BUSY PERSON CAN? Some of us do. Canning sounds old-fashioned, laborious, and difficult. In fact, although it is more time-consuming than freezing and more labor-intensive than root cellaring or drying, it is not difficult. Also, nothing beats the convenience of having canned tomatoes ready to turn into an instant sauce, or opening a jar of applesauce or sugar-free peaches as an instant snack for hungry kids. If you are planning to make pickles, jams, or salsas, you will find that canning is necessary for the best finished product. So while you may not need to know how to can to preserve most vegetables, having the technique in your repertoire will give you the most variety in your pantry.

In this book I focus on boiling-water-bath canning, suitable for high-acid fruits and vegetables and pickles. I will also show you two methods of packing jars — raw-pack and hot-pack. If you are interested in pressure canning, the only acceptable method for low-acid vegetables, consult your local Extension Service agent or a preserving book that includes more advanced methods.

CANNING JARS AND LIDS

Use only ½-pint, pint, 1½-pint, and quart jars made especially for canning. Commercial jars, such as the type mayonnaise comes in, are too thin and will not withstand the heat required for processing vegetables. European-made jars cannot be used with our time charts because they are calibrated in metric sizes. Make sure your jars are free from nicks and cracks.

Although you can still find old-fashioned lids at garage sales, the modern two-piece screw band and lid is the type of lid you will most likely work with, and it is the safest. These must be used with threaded jars. The metal lids have a flanged edge with a rubberlike compound on them that seals to

two-piece screw band and lid

the edge of the jar. The lid is held in place with a screw band during processing. After the jars have been sealed, the screw band should be removed. The band can be reused to process other jars, but the lids are not reusable.

PREPARING JARS AND LIDS

Wash enough jars for several batches of food all at once. A dishwasher comes in handy for this job. Place the jars upside down on clean towels in a clean area. They will be ready when you have time to can.

If your jars have not been prewashed, wash and rinse them when you are setting up. Check for chips and cracks that might have occurred during washing.

To heat jars and keep them hot for canning, fill a roasting pan with water, set it in the oven at 200°F, and leave the jars in the water until you need them. You can also heat jars by keeping them in the dishwasher on the dry cycle. Jars that will be filled with food and processed for 10 minutes or less, as for jams and jellies and some pickles, must be sterilized beforehand by completely submerging them in a boiling- water bath for a full 10 minutes.

Place jar lids and screw bands in water according to the manufacturer's directions.

TIPS ON WASHING VEGETABLES

Wash vegetables in plenty of cold water. Use a medium stiff-bristled brush or a plastic or nylon net scrubber that can get into the crevices where the dirt is hardest to remove. A stiff-bristled brush will just skim over these areas. Be especially thorough with root crops since botulism bacteria may be in the soil, and only thorough washing will remove them from the vegetables. Always lift vegetables out of the water rather than letting water drain off; otherwise the dirt will be redeposited on them.

RAW-PACK VERSUS HOT-PACK

Raw-pack. Raw-pack is sometimes erroneously referred to as cold-pack, but that reference is misleading. Raw-pack means packing prepared vegetables and fruit into the canning jar raw. This method is the fastest way to pack since it does not require heated jars or precooked food. Cleanup is faster because you do not have the extra pans and utensils to wash.

Are there disadvantages to raw-packing? Some shrinkage will occur, and occasionally the fruits or vegetables (especially tomatoes) will float to the top of the jar. Plus, the jars will hold slightly less when packed this way, and entrapped air may cause discoloration of the food after 2 to 3 months of storage. But I don't think these drawbacks outweigh the ease of preparation and the time savings of this method.

Hot-pack. To hot-pack a jar, precook your food as described for specific types; then pack the hot foods loosely into hot jars. Obviously, this method is more time-consuming than the raw-pack method.

SEALING JARS

With the modern two-piece screw bands and lids, you will have to buy new lids each time you process. Follow the manufacturer's directions for sealing.

When processing time is complete, remove the jars from the canner and place them several inches apart on a towel. Do not tighten screw bands on jars with the two-piece screw bands and lids.

Do not open any jar, even if liquid has boiled out. The food is safe as long as it was processed properly and the jar seals properly.

Do not cover the jars while they are cooling. Allow the jars to cool for 24 hours; then test the seal.

> tip ❖ Salt is added to canned vegetables for taste. It is not necessary for any other reason.

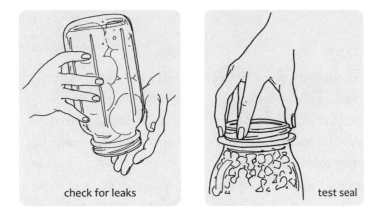

check for leaks

test seal

TESTING SEALS

After the cooling period is completed, remove the screw bands on jars with two-piece lids to prevent them from rusting onto the jars and to help you detect broken seals.

What does a good seal look like? The lid should be depressed in the center, and if you pick the jar up by the edge of the lid, it will not come loose. With the jar tipped upside down, check for any leaks. If you find any leaks, or if the center of the jar lid pops back, refrigerate that jar to use within a few days, or reprocess.

To reprocess, clean the rim of the jar. Add liquid, if necessary, to maintain the proper headspace, and put on a new lid and screw band. Then reprocess as before, for the full length of time recommended.

Basic
Techniques
for
Preserving
Food

53

> tip ✿ Make use of leisure time by chopping and dicing vegetables while watching your favorite show on television. Use a cutting board that fits in your lap, and put the diced vegetables in a large plastic bag as you dice or cut them. Divide them into smaller bags later, or tray-freeze and package in larger bags.

STORING JARS

Store jars in a cool, dark place, where they will not freeze. Warm temperatures cause discoloration and taste changes, and could cause spoilage that would not otherwise occur. Freezing does not make food unsafe, unless the jar is cracked or the cap loosened; but some foods may soften in texture.

Before using a jar of home-canned food, check for signs of spoilage. Bulging or unsealed lids, spurting liquid, mold, malodorous contents, or a constant stream of tiny bubbles when the jar is turned upside down indicate spoilage. Some bubbles are normal; but if after the contents have settled, you can see a continual flow of tiny bubbles from around the lid of the jar, then you must discard the contents. Discard the food from any jars that look suspicious, disposing of it where humans or animals will not eat it. Wash the jars well with hot, sudsy water and boil them for 15 minutes before using them again.

tips ✣ Acid foods, including all fruits, tomatoes (to which you added lemon juice or citric acid), rhubarb, sauerkraut, and pickled foods, can be safely processed in a boiling-water bath. Low-acid foods include all vegetables except tomatoes, and all other foods that do not fall into the acid group, such as meat. Low-acid foods must be processed in a pressure canner.

✣ To remove a stuck screw band, wring out a cloth in hot water, and then wrap it around the band for a minute or so to help loosen it.

✣ To prevent hard-water mineral stains on jars and build-up in canners, use ½ cup vinegar per canner-full of hard water.

BOILING-WATER-BATH CANNING: Fifteen Steps

Boiling-water-bath canning is the USDA's recommended way of canning acid foods — fruits, pickles, and acidified tomatoes. With a boiling-water-bath canner, you immerse jars of food in hot water to cover and begin counting the processing time once the water begins to boil.

1 Make sure your work area and all equipment are spotlessly clean. If your jars have not been prewashed, wash and rinse them. Check the jars for nicks and cracks. If you plan to hot-pack, keep the jars hot in water.

Assemble your equipment and set your tools where they will be most convenient. You will need a scrub brush, a colander and/or strainer, paring and chopping knives, a cutting board, food processing equipment, measuring cups and spoons, a bubble expeller (wooden chopsticks work well), a widemouthed funnel, large bowls, canning jars, a boiling-water-bath canner, a preserving kettle, a teakettle filled with hot water, canning lids and screw bands, large wooden and slotted spoons, a soup ladle, a jar lifter or tongs, a timer, hot pads, mitts or heavy potholders, and towels.

2 Fill your canner with about 4 inches of water for pints and 4½ inches for quarts. (These amounts are for a 20- to 21-quart canner.) Place the canner on the stove and begin heating. Heat extra water to boiling in a teakettle.

heat water in canner

3 Wash your jars in soapy water, rinse well, and then keep hot by placing the jars in the preheating canner or in a dishwasher. If processing for 10 minutes or less, as for jams and jellies, sterilize the jars by boiling for 10 minutes in the canner. Leave the jars in the water until you are ready to process.

4 Place the jar lids and screw bands in water according to the manufacturer's directions.

5 Select perfect fruits and vegetables at the peak of their maturity. Wash the produce. Drain.

6 Prepare the vegetables for pickling or canning: peel, slice, dice, julienne, or leave whole.

7 Pack the jars.

Raw-pack. Firmly pack clean, heated jars with fruits or vegetables. If desired, add ½ teaspoon salt to pints, 1 teaspoon to quarts. Fill the jars with hot, not boiling, water, syrup, or juice, leaving the proper headspace, as noted in the recipe.

Hot-pack. Place prepared tomatoes, fruit, purée, or juice in a large pan; cover fruit with syrup or juice. Bring to a boil and simmer tomato products for 5 minutes, fruit for 3 minutes. Pack loosely into clean, hot jars, adding ½ teaspoon salt to pints and 1 teaspoon to quarts, if desired. Fill jars of whole tomatoes or fruit with hot liquid, leaving the recommended headspace.

8 Expel air bubbles in the jar by running a nonmetallic kitchen utensil gently between the vegetables and jar. Add more liquid if necessary to maintain the proper headspace.

9 Wipe the rim of the jar with a clean, damp cloth, and seal.

10 When the jars are packed and the lids are in place, check the canner. If the water is boiling, add cold water to reduce the temperature enough

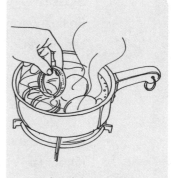

place lids in water

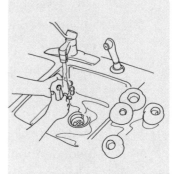

wash produce

pack jars

expel air bubbles

wipe rim

lower jar into canner

(140°F for raw-pack foods and 180°F for hot-pack foods) to cushion the shock of adding the cooler jars to the boiling water.

Carefully lower the jars, using long-handled tongs or a jar lifter, into the hot water in the canner. Be careful not to bump jars against one another as you lower the rack; this could cause jars to crack. Water should cover jars by 2 full inches. If necessary, add more boiling water to the canner.

11 Start counting the processing time required in the recipe as soon as the water returns to a full boil. Keep the water at a full boil throughout the processing time. (A teakettle of boiling water should be kept on hand to replenish the water in the canner, if necessary.) See the chart on page 58 if you are processing at an altitude above 1,000 feet.

12 If you are canning more than one batch of food, prepare the second batch while the first is processing. While the last batch is processing, clean your work area.

13 When processing time is up, turn off the heat, carefully remove the cover from the canner, and wait 5 minutes to help ensure proper sealing and avoid boil-overs from the jars. Using long-handled tongs or jar lifters, carefully remove jars from the canner. Place the jars several inches apart on a towel away from drafts.

If the screw bands are loose, do not tighten them.

Basic
Techniques
for
Preserving
Food

remove jars to heavy towel

check seal

14 Cool the jars for 24 hours. After the cooling period is completed, remove the screw bands and check the seals. Wipe the sealed jars with a clean, damp cloth. Then label clearly with the product and date.

15 Store the jars in a cool, dark, dry place where they will not freeze.

If you live at an altitude above 1,000 feet, you will need to increase the processing time as indicated below:

ELEVATION	ADJUSTMENT
1,001 to 3,000 feet	Add 5 minutes to the processing time
3,001 to 6,000 feet	Add 10 minutes to the processing time
6,001 to 8,000 feet	Add 15 minutes to the processing time
Above 8,000 feet	Add 20 minutes to the processing time

Chapter 4

Preserving Vegetables

THERE IS A *BEST* WAY TO PRESERVE each vegetable;
there is *a fastest* way as well — and sometimes the best way
is the fastest way, but not always. The best way means that
the vegetable will taste closest to fresh when you cook it for
the table.

Suppose your beans are ready to harvest. Turn to the page
on beans in this chapter. Decide which preservation method
to use. Does it look like you will have enough time to get the
job done? Fine. Then read the harvest tips for beans, and go
into the garden and pick the beans. What if you don't have
enough time to process the beans? Those beans are going to
get too mature out in the garden. You don't want to wait to
pick them.

IN CHAPTER 2, I shared some of the different shortcuts I have used in my kitchen — such as storing fresh vegetables overnight in garbage cans filled with ice or tray-freezing unblanched beans to be used later in relishes. Check the index or skim through chapter 2 to find shortcuts that will work for you.

Before you start freezing, drying, or canning, turn back to chapter 3 for a quick review of the basic techniques. Assembling all your equipment, setting up for a productive work flow, and ensuring the safety of your methods will help to save you time in the long run.

With the basic techniques fresh in your mind, follow the step-by-step instructions I have provided for each vegetable.

Ready to harvest? Let's start with asparagus.

ASPARAGUS

ASPARAGUS SHOULD BE PICKED when it is 6 to 8 inches high and thicker than a pencil. During harvesting, all shoots should be cut. Leaving the smaller shoots to grow will shorten the harvest season, which can continue for 6 to 10 weeks.

Freezing in Boilable Bags
Best and quickest method

① Begin heating water for blanching. To prepare the asparagus, wash by scrubbing gently (asparagus is delicate) with a vegetable brush to remove any sand. Cut off tough ends or snap at the brittle point. Cut into pieces or sort spears. Pack in boilable bags. Add butter and seasonings, if desired. Press out air. Seal bags.

② Blanch bags, four at a time, in boiling water for 4 to 8 minutes, depending on size.

③ Cool. Pat bags dry. Freeze.

> **cooking tip ❖** To cook vegetables frozen in boilable bags in the microwave, place the bag on a microwave-safe plate or bowl. Cut a ½-inch slit in the top of the bag. Microwave on HIGH (100% power) for 4 to 6 minutes. Quarter-turn the dish halfway through the cooking, if necessary. Leave the vegetables in the bag for an additional 4 to 5 minutes, then serve.

Freezing the Standard Way

① Begin heating water for blanching in a steamer. Scrub gently with a vegetable brush to remove any sand. Cut off tough ends or snap at the brittle point. Cut into pieces or sort spears.

② Steam-blanch, 1 pound at a time for 3 to 6 minutes, depending on size.

③ Cool in ice water. Drain. Pack. Press out air. Seal. Freeze.

BEANS: GREEN

THE BEST BEANS FOR PRESERVING are those that are slightly immature. Green beans should be long and slender and have tiny seeds. Harvest beans late in the day. The foliage should be dry. Harvesting beans from wet plants may cause the developing crop to rot.

Beans can be left to dry on the vine past maturity. After the pods are dry, shell them. Dry the beans on cookie sheets for several days. Place the beans in airtight containers and store in a dry place. These beans may be used as regular dried beans in soups and casseroles.

Can't preserve right away? Do not wash beans. Store by one of the methods suggested in chapter 3.

Preserving
Vegetables

61

Freezing Unblanched Whole or Julienne Beans

🍃 *Best and quickest method*

① Trim ends of beans.

② Wash, drain, pat thoroughly dry. Julienne, if desired.

③ Pack in gallon-size freezer bags. Press out air. Seal. Freeze.

Note: Unblanched beans will retain good quality for 6 months.

trim bean ends

drain on towel

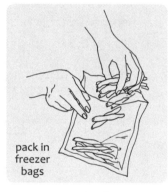

pack in freezer bags

tip ✿ Another excellent way to preserve beans is to pickle them. You'll find a recipe for Dilly Beans on page 146.

cooking tip ✿ Frozen beans should be cooked by steaming or stir-frying for best flavor and texture, or cooked in the boilable bag for 18 to 20 minutes. The less contact beans have with water during freezing and cooking, the better flavor and texture they will have.

Freezing in Boilable Bags

① Begin heating water for blanching. To prepare the beans, trim the ends. Wash, drain, pat dry. Pack in boilable bags. Add butter and seasonings, if desired. Press out air. Seal bags.

② Blanch bags, four at a time, in boiling water: 6 minutes for young beans, up to 8 minutes for old beans.

③ Cool. Pat bags dry. Freeze.

Freezing the Standard Way

① Trim the ends from the beans. Begin heating water for blanching. Wash the beans, drain.

② Steam-blanch, 1 pound at a time: 4½ minutes for young beans, 6 minutes for old beans.

③ Cool in ice water. Drain. Pack. Press out air. Seal. Freeze.

BEETS

BEETS SHOULD BE LEFT IN THE GARDEN UNTIL LATE FALL. A few frosts will not harm them. Dig beets on a sunny day. Cut the tops off, leaving an inch of stem. Do not cut off roots. Let the beets lie on the ground until the following day. Beets stored in a root cellar will remain fresh and taste sweet well into late spring.

> tip ❖ Beets are good candidates for pickling. You'll find a recipe on page 147.

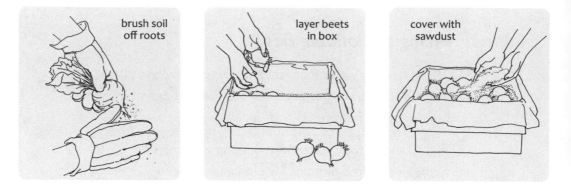

brush soil off roots

layer beets in box

cover with sawdust

Storing in a Root Cellar
✒ Best and quickest method

① Brush off the excess soil on the roots, but do not wash. Place a large plastic bag in a cardboard box; add 2 to 4 inches of fresh sawdust (2 inches for storage areas that will remain above freezing).

② Add a single layer of beets, leaving a 2-inch space all around the side of the layer to be filled with sawdust. Cover with a 1-inch layer of sawdust. Continue to layer the beets until the box is full. Finish with a 2- to 4-inch layer of sawdust.

③ Fold over the top of the bag and close the box. Store in the coldest part of the root cellar or in an unheated area, such as a garage.

tip ✣ One method of peeling beets is to cut the tops from beets, leaving 2 inches of stem to prevent bleeding. Do not cut the roots off. Scrub thoroughly. Place in a large kettle. Cover with hot tap water. Bring to a boil and boil for 15 to 20 minutes for canned beets, or until tender for frozen beets. Slip off skins. The disadvantage of this method is that the beets should all be the same size; otherwise, smaller beets will overcook and get mushy before larger ones are cooked. This problem does not happen when beets are baked in the oven; beets of several sizes may be baked together and none overcook.

Freezing Slices in Boilable Bags

① Cut tops and roots off close to the beet. Preheat oven to 400°F. Scrub beets thoroughly. Place on a rack in a large roaster. Cover.

② Bake until tender (approximately 1 hour for 2½- to 3-inch beets).

③ Fill the roaster with cold water to cool beets. Slip off skins.

④ Slice beets. Pack in boilable freezer bags. Add butter and seasoning, if desired. Press out air. Seal.

⑤ Cool in ice water. Wipe dry. Freeze.

BROCCOLI

HARVEST BROCCOLI WHEN THE HEAD STOPS GROWING but before the individual clusters start to spread out. Second crop clusters (side shoots) should be cut while the buds are still clustered tightly.

Can't preserve right away? Do not wash. Store by one of the methods suggested in chapter 2.

Freezing the Standard Way
☙ *Best method*

① Soak broccoli in cold, salted water for ½ hour to remove dirt and insects. Meanwhile, preheat water for steam-blanching.

② Drain broccoli. Rinse. Divide into uniform-size pieces or chop.

③ Steam-blanch, 1 pound at a time for 5 minutes. Then cool, drain, pack, press out air, and seal. Freeze.

> tip ✴ When blanching broccoli, make long cross cuts in the stalk, so that the stalk will cook in the same length of time as the bud.

Freezing Unblanched Broccoli

✎ *Quickest method*

① Soak broccoli in cold, salted water for 30 minutes to remove dirt and insects. Rinse well. Drain. Divide into uniform-size pieces or chop.

② Pack in gallon-size freezer bags. Press out air. Seal. Freeze.

> cooking tip ❋ For best flavor and texture, frozen broccoli should be steamed or stir-fried.

soak in salted water

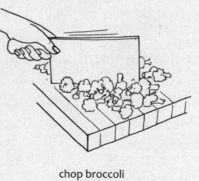
chop broccoli

pack into freezer bags

> tip ❋ Unblanched broccoli florets retain good quality in the freezer for only 6 weeks, while the stalks hold up for 3 months. Save time by freezing sliced pieces of stalks without blanching, and blanch the florets for the best finished product. The sliced stalks make an excellent addition to mixed stir-fried vegetables.

CABBAGE

CABBAGE FOR WINTER keeping should be left in the garden as late in the fall as possible. Pick just before the first frost. If the heads indicate a tendency to split, and it's too early to harvest, give the heads a quarter turn to break off some of the roots; this will slow down the growth and can be repeated every 7 to 10 days. When ready to harvest, pull the entire plant up from the garden, roots and all.

pull cabbage with roots

Storing in a Root Cellar

🖎 *Best and quickest method*

① Pull up cabbage plants with roots intact.

② Transfer freshly pulled cabbage plants directly to the root cellar, and hang upside down on hooks or nails.

③ Retain the outer leaves; they will form a dry paperlike covering that will help to keep the cabbage fresh.

hang to dry

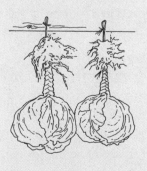

retain leaves on heads

Preserving
Vegetables

67

tips ❖ Finely shredded cabbage can be made into the freezer coleslaw on page 149.

❖ Cabbage can be brined as sauerkraut or made into relishes; for recipes see chapter 7.

❖ Outer leaves of cabbage can be frozen whole and unblanched to be used as wrappers for baked stuffed cabbage leaves. Since the leaves will wilt when defrosted, it will not be necessary to drop them into boiling water before preparing this dish.

❖ Coarsely chopped cabbage can be frozen unblanched to be used in soups or casserole dishes within 4 to 6 months. Steam-cook frozen cabbage for casserole dishes requiring cooked cabbage.

CARROTS

CARROTS SHOULD BE LEFT IN THE GARDEN UNTIL you are ready to store or process them. Carrots for cold storage are best if harvested late in the fall, though they should not be allowed to become oversized and stringy. A few light frosts will not harm them. Carrots stored in a root cellar will remain fresh and taste sweet well into late spring.

Storing in a Root Cellar
❧ *Best and quickest method*

① Dig carrots on a sunny day; cut off tops close to the carrot and let them lie on the ground all day or even overnight to kill the little feeder roots. Do not wash the carrots.

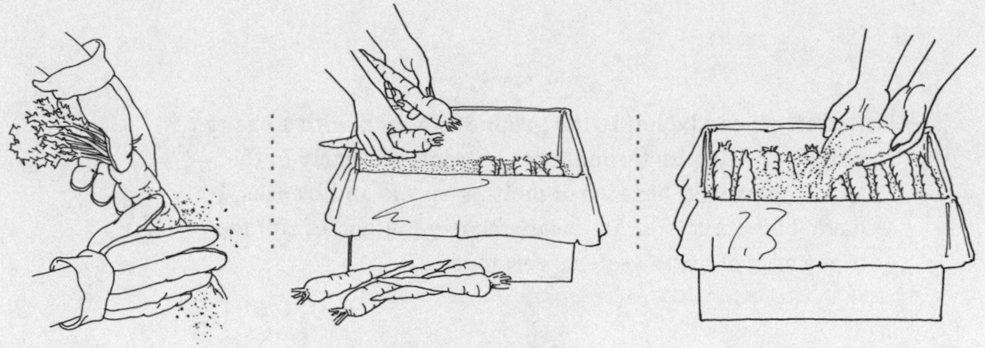

brush soil off carrots — layer carrots in box — cover with sawdust

② Brush off excess soil. Place a large plastic bag in a cardboard box; add 2 to 4 inches of fresh sawdust (2 inches for storage areas that will remain above freezing). Add a single layer of carrots, leaving a 2-inch space all around the sides of the box to be filled with sawdust. Cover with a 1-inch layer of sawdust. Continue until box is full, finishing with a 2- to 4-inch layer of sawdust.

③ Fold over top of the bag and close the box. Store in the coldest area of the root cellar or an unheated area such as a garage.

tip ✲ Mature fall carrots result in a better frozen product than young early carrots. They should be peeled before freezing.

Freezing in Boilable Bags

① Begin heating water for blanching. Scrub carrots thoroughly; peel. Slice or julienne with a food processor.

② Pack in boilable bags. Add butter and seasonings, if desired. Press out air. Seal.

③ Blanch bags, four at a time, in boiling water for 8 to 10 minutes.

④ Cool. Pat bags dry. Freeze.

tip ❖ Carrots can be left in the ground, covered with a heavy mulch, and dug up throughout the winter or early in the spring; however, because of melting snows and freezes, I have found this to be an unsatisfactory method of storage in my area of northwestern Vermont.

Freezing the Standard Way

① Scrub carrots thoroughly; peel. Begin heating water for blanching. Slice or julienne carrots with a food processor. Whole carrots do not freeze well.

② Blanch, 1 pound at a time, by steam or immersion, for 3 to 4 minutes.

③ Cool. Drain well. Pack. Press out air. Seal. Freeze.

CORN

HARVEST YOUR CORN as soon as the kernels become full and sweet. Corn is at the right stage for picking when you can press milky fluid from the kernels. If the fluid is too clear, the corn is not ready; if it is thick, the corn has gone past its prime and will taste tough and starchy. Starchy corn is best used in cream-style corn.

Some of the newer hybrid, supersweet varieties will retain their prime flavor up to 4 days, if left right on the stalk. Others should be picked as soon as they are ready. Be sure you know which type you planted.

If you must harvest corn before you are ready to process it, harvest it late in the afternoon and do not husk. Place the corn in a large barrel with a layer of ice between each layer of ears. Cover with several layers of newspaper and a lid, if possible. Corn will keep this way for about 24 hours before losing its sweet flavor.

place corn on cookie sheets

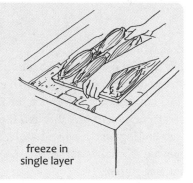
freeze in
single layer

place corn
in bag

Freezing Unblanched Corn in Husks
🖐 *Quickest method*

① Harvest the corn, and do not husk. Place the ears on cookie sheets, or just put them in the freezer loose in a single layer. Freeze for 48 hours.

② Bag the corn in a large, plastic food-safe bag.

③ Return to freezer. Remove ears as needed. Eat within 4 months.

> cooking tip ❄ To cook corn frozen in husks, husk the frozen corn under cold running water. Remove the silks by rotating your hands around the corn. Put the corn in a pan; cover with cool water. Cover the pan, heat to boiling, and boil for 1 minute. Remove from heat, and let the corn stand in hot water for 5 minutes. Eat immediately.

Preserving
Vegetables

71

Freezing Corn on the Cob in Boilable Bags
🖐 *Best method*

① Begin heating water for blanching. Husk cobs, trim, and pack in boilable bags. Add butter if desired. Press out air. Seal.

② Blanch bags, four at a time, in boiling water, for 10 minutes. After 5 minutes, turn bags over.

③ Cool in ice water. Pat bags dry. Freeze.

Freezing Corn on the Cob the Standard Way

① Husk cobs. Begin heating water for blanching. Trim.

② Blanch six ears at a time by steam for 10½ to 16½ minutes or by immersion for 7 to 11 minutes.

③ Cool. Drain. Pack in bags. Press out air. Seal. Freeze.

Freezing Cream-Style Corn

① Husk. Cut corn from the cob by cutting down through the center of the kernel. Scrape remaining corn from the cob.

② Measure kernels as you pour into a large kettle. Add ¼ cup boiling water and 1 teaspoon cornstarch per cup. Stir well. Bring to a boil; reduce heat and simmer for 5 minutes, stirring frequently. Fill sink with ice water while cooking corn.

③ Place kettle in sink of ice water. Stir to cool.

④ Package in rigid containers or bags; freeze.

Whole Kernel Corn in Boilable Bags
❧ *Best and quickest method for kernels*

① Husk. Begin heating water for blanching. Cut corn from the cob. Pack in boilable bags. Add butter if desired. Press out air. Seal bags.

② Blanch bags, four at a time, in boiling water for 6 minutes.

③ Cool. Pat bags dry. Freeze.

CUCUMBERS

CUCUMBERS CAN BE PICKED AT ANY STAGE: tiny, for whole pickles; medium, for dill, sliced, or chunk pickles; large, for ripe cucumber pickles. For eating fresh, cucumbers should be harvested when they are 4 to 6 inches long and about 1 to 1½ inches in diameter.

Cucumbers cannot be canned or frozen by any of the regular methods; they must be preserved in brine or vinegar, or frozen for salads. Thinly sliced and frozen in brine, they produce a delightful, fresh, crisp flavor to be used in salads all winter.

When cucumbers have reached just the right stage for a specific type of pickle, they should be picked immediately. Even 1 day can allow too much growth. Do not wash cucumbers; store by one of the methods suggested in chapter 2.

Preserving Vegetables

73

slice cucumbers thinly

mix with onions and salt

rinse vegetables

Freezing Slices for Salads
🥬 Quickest method

① Wash 6 to 8 firm, slender cucumbers. Slice thinly with a food processor. Peel and thinly slice 1 medium-size onion. Measure out 2 quarts of sliced cucumbers. Mix with onions and 2 tablespoons of salt in a large bowl.

② Let stand for 2 hours.

③ Drain vegetables well. Rinse thoroughly with cold water. Drain well again. Return drained vegetables to the rinsed bowl. Add ⅔ cup each of oil, vinegar, and sugar. Add 1 teaspoon celery seed. Mix well.

pack into freezer boxes

④ Cover and refrigerate overnight.

⑤ Pack in freezer jars or rigid freezer containers. Leave 1-inch headspace. Freeze.

tip ❉ Cucumber slices can be defrosted and eaten after 1 week. Store defrosted cucumbers in refrigerator for up to 2 weeks.

EGGPLANT

IGNORE THE SIZE OF THE FRUIT when it comes to harvesting egg-plant. Depending on the variety, climate, and soil conditions, your eggplant may vary in size from several inches to a foot or more. The thing to look for is a glossy shine on the skin.

Can't preserve right away? Because eggplant has a fairly neutral flavor and a texture that is so radically altered in cooking, it is per-fectly acceptable to store eggplant in a cool place for several days before preserving, provided you harvested when the fruit was firm and glossy, not dull-colored and soft. You will get best results freez-ing eggplant in your favorite eggplant casserole. Bake the casserole until almost done in a dish lined with aluminum foil; cool and freeze. When frozen solid, remove the dish and leave the casserole wrapped in foil or freezer wrap. When ready to use, unwrap, put back into the original dish, and bake until done. Or freeze in a microwave-safe casserole dish, and when ready to use, defrost and heat in the micro-wave. (For a recipe, see page 192.)

Freezing the Standard Way
Best and quickest method

① Begin heating 1 gallon water for blanching. Add ¼ cup lemon juice to water to prevent discoloration. Peel the eggplant and cut into slices ½ inch thick.

② Blanch, 1 pound at a time, for 4 minutes.

③ Cool in ice water. Drain. Pat dry. Pack. Press out air. Seal. Freeze.

GREENS

SPINACH TO BE PRESERVED should be harvested when the leafy portion is 6 inches long. Chard and other greens should be harvested while still young and tender. Chard can be as long as 10 inches. Spinach bolts and turns bitter quickly when the weather warms up, so watch it carefully. Greens should be harvested early in the day while dew is still on the leaves and before the warming rays of the sun cause them to go limp. If cut at this point, they will stay fresh for as long as 2 to 3 days.

chop greens

Can't preserve right away? Do not wash greens. Store by one of the methods suggested in chapter 2. Avoid placing heavy packages of ice on top of the tender leaves.

Stir-Fry Greens
🍃 *Best and quickest method*

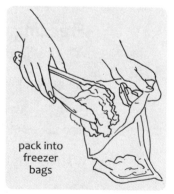
stir-fry until wilted

① Wash, pick over, drain. Cut through with large knife.

② Stir-fry until wilted, 2 to 3 minutes.

③ Pack in boilable bags.

④ Cool. Pat bags dry. Freeze.

pack into freezer bags

76

> tip ✤ Fresh greens can be frozen by using the standard method of freezing. That method takes more time, and since the product is not as good, I do not recommend it.

LETTUCE

LATE-PLANTED FALL LETTUCE can be harvested right up until the first frost.

transplant lettuce into cold frame

Extending the Harvest

① To preserve lettuce for winter use, plant seed in the garden in late summer.

② Transplant to a cold frame just before the first frost.

③ Properly cared for, lettuce will continue to produce well into the early winter.

MUSHROOMS

A BOUNTY OF WILD MUSHROOMS or a great buy on mushrooms at the store may tempt you to preserve them. Mushrooms can be dried or frozen — just be sure to use commercially grown varieties or those that you know beyond any doubt are nontoxic.

Another simple way to preserve mushrooms is to cook them by sautéing in butter or oil, cooling, then packing in freezer containers.

Preserving
Vegetables

tips ✾ To use dried mushrooms, place in a bowl, pour in boiling water to cover, and let soak for 20 to 30 minutes.

✾ To rehydrate dried vegetables quickly, place them in a microwave-safe bowl, cover with cold water, and stir to make sure the vegetables are immersed in the water. Cover and microwave on HIGH (100% power) just to the boiling point. Remove from the oven and let sit until the vegetables are tender.

Drying Mushrooms
✐ Best and quickest method

① Wash mushrooms quickly in cold water, without soaking or peeling. Trim ⅛ inch off stem end. Thinly slice or finely chop.

② Dry in a dehydrator at 120°F for 8 to 12 hours, stirring occasionally and rotating trays once or twice. Well-dried mushrooms should be tough and leathery with no sign of moisture in the center. Or dry in a conventional oven at 120°F for 12 to 18 hours, stirring occasionally and rotating trays once or twice, until the mushrooms are leathery and tough.

③ Cool and package in airtight containers.

Freezing the Standard Way

① Begin preheating water for blanching. Wash mushrooms quickly in cold water, without soaking or peeling. Trim ⅛ inch off stem end. Leave whole or slice as desired.

② Blanch, 1 pound at a time: 3 minutes for sliced mushrooms, 5 minutes for whole.

③ Cool mushrooms in ice water. Drain. Pack. Press out air. Seal. Freeze.

ONIONS, GARLIC, AND SHALLOTS

ALL MEMBERS OF THE SAME FAMILY, onions, garlic, and shallots are the easiest vegetables to harvest and store. Wait until their tops have fallen over in the late summer or early fall and the stems have almost completely dried. Do not try to hasten maturity by bending over the tops before they are ready to fall themselves.

pack in mesh bags

or braid
and hang

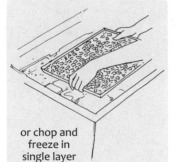

or chop and
freeze in
single layer

Pull the onions up and allow them to dry in the sun. The longer they are dried before storage, the better they will keep. As a rule of thumb, I never put my onions in storage until the outer skins are totally dry and slip off easily — usually 2 to 3 weeks. I dry my onions on an old screen door that has been placed across sawhorses. This placement speeds the drying process and prevents rot that could be caused by a week of constant rains.

While cold storage is the easiest and fastest method of storage, having a supply of chopped frozen or dried onions is a great convenience for meal preparation on busy nights.

One pound of onions can be peeled and chopped in a food processor in 5 minutes. If your supply of stored onions begins to sprout in the spring, tray-freezing or drying the remainder of the crop will prevent a waste of good food.

Storing in a Root Cellar
🌿 *Best and quickest method*

The fastest and easiest method of storing dried onions, garlic, and shallots is to pack them into mesh bags and store in a cool, dry area. The next best method is to braid them before the stems are completely dried. Finish drying out in the sun and store in a cool, dry area. It takes me approximately 15 minutes to braid a foot-long string of onions.

Preserving
Vegetables

79

tip ✿ Do not store onions in humid areas. They tolerate cold temperatures as low as 38°F quite well but will spoil quickly if the humidity is high.

Tray-Freezing Unblanched Chopped Onions

① Peel and chop or slice onions.

② Spread in a single layer on baking sheets and tray-freeze.

③ Package frozen onions within 12 to 24 hours.

> tip ❖ Freeze a mixture of onions and green or moderately hot peppers to be fried and eaten with hamburgers or frankfurters.

Drying Chopped Onions

① Peel and chop onions.

② Dry in a dehydrator at 120°F for 12 to 24 hours, stirring occasionally and rotating trays once or twice after the first 8 hours, until brittle. Or dry in a conventional oven at 120°F for 24 to 36 hours, stirring occasionally and rotating trays once or twice, until brittle.

③ Cool and package in airtight containers.

PEAS

GREEN PEAS SHOULD BE HARVESTED as soon as the peas fill the pod. Older peas lose their sweetness quickly and become tough. Harvest from the bottom of the plant first, since these are first to mature. Pick peas late in the afternoon for sweetest flavor. Snow peas must be picked before the pea seed starts to develop. Sugar snap peas can be picked at any stage, right up until they fill the pod tightly, to freeze for stir-frying, which is the only cooking method I recommend for this variety. If you can't preserve right away, chill your peas immediately by storing according to one of the methods suggested in chapter 2.

> tip ✿ Peas that go past maturity can be left to dry on the vine. Shell and store in dry airtight containers to use in soups.

Freezing the Standard Way
Excellent finished product

1. Shell peas. Preheat water for steam-blanching. Wash peas. Drain.

2. Blanch, 1 pound at a time, for 3 minutes.

3. Cool peas in ice water. Drain. Pack. Press out air. Seal. Freeze.

Preserving
Vegetables

Freezing Peas in a Boilable Bag
🐭 *Best and quickest method*

① Begin heating water for blanching. Shell peas, wash, and drain. Pack in 1-pint boilable freezer bags. Add butter and seasoning, if desired. Press out air. Seal.

② Blanch, four bags at a time, in boiling water for 4 minutes.

③ Cool bags in ice water. Pat dry. Freeze.

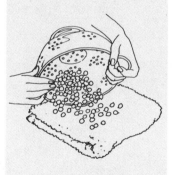

drain peas on towel

blanch boilable bag

chill in ice water

cooking tip ❋ Peas packed in boilable freezer bags can be cooked in the bag in boiling water for 20 minutes. Loosely packed peas are best when steam-cooked until barely tender, 5 to 8 minutes.

Blanching and Tray-Freezing Snow and Sugar Snap Peas

🌱 *Best and quickest method*

steam-blanch peas

① Preheat water for steam-blanching. Wash. Trim ends off pods and remove strings.

② Steam-blanch, 1 pound at a time, for 2 to 4½ minutes.

③ Cool peas in ice water. Drain.

④ Pat dry. Tray-freeze.

⑤ When frozen solid, pack in large freezer bags or containers.

freeze in single layer

cooking tips ❋ Snow peas and sugar snap peas do not retain their crisp texture when frozen; cook by stir-frying.

❋ Frozen sugar snap peas can be chopped and put in tossed salads while still frozen. If they are added just 3 to 4 minutes before the salad is served, they will be crisp, cold, and sweet.

pack into freezer bag

Preserving Vegetables

SWEET PEPPERS

FOR THE BEST FROZEN OR DRIED PRODUCT, peppers should be picked when they are fully mature in size and have thick flesh. Since peppers keep well on the bush, there is no need to pick until you are ready to use them. As peppers go past the initial stage of maturity, they will sweeten and turn red. This does not affect the quality or texture of the vegetable, and red peppers add nice color to soups and casseroles. Peppers can be stored in the refrigerator for up to 2 weeks.

Peppers are a good candidate for drying. While the quickest way to prepare them for drying is to simply cut each in half and deseed, I find it more convenient to use dried diced peppers. Pepper halves must be rehydrated in boiling water for 30 to 45 minutes before using in a recipe, but diced pieces can be added to soups, stews, or rice as it cooks, without any further preparation.

remove stem and membrane

Tray-Freezing Peppers Whole or in Halves

🍂 *Best and quickest method*

① Wash; cut out stem end, seed pod, and white membrane.

② Tray-freeze whole or cut in half.

③ Package frozen peppers within 12 to 24 hours.

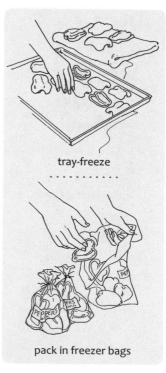

tray-freeze

pack in freezer bags

cooking tip ❈ Whole or half peppers prepared this way can be stuffed and baked; or sliced, diced, or ground from the frozen state, as needed.

Drying Diced Peppers
☞ *Excellent finished product*

① Wash; cut out stem end, seed pod, and white membrane. Dice or chop.

② Dry in a dehydrator at 120°F for 8 to 12 hours, stirring occasionally and rotating trays once or twice. Or dry in a conventional oven at 120°F for 18 to 24 hours, stirring occasionally and rotating trays once, until leathery with no moisture inside.

③ Cool and package in airtight containers.

POTATOES

POTATOES FOR WINTER keeping should not be dug until the tops die off. Once the tops have died, pull the tops from the ground 10 days before digging. This will prevent diseases from starting that could destroy the tubers. Do not wash potatoes before storing. After digging potatoes, store at normal temperatures (60°F to 75°F) for 10 to 14 days to let the skins dry out enough to prevent moisture loss. The storage area should be protected from light as much as possible; otherwise, potatoes will develop solanine (manifested as a green coloring on the surface), and this condition can cause illness.

Preserving
Vegetables

85

If you do a lot of backpacking, you may want to consider drying some of your potato harvest. Dried potatoes must be watched carefully, however, for any hint of moisture will cause the entire batch to mold. To use, pour 1 cup of boiling water over 1 cup of dried potatoes. Cook 45 to 50 minutes for boiled potatoes or hash browns. One cup dried potatoes yields 1 to 1½ cups cooked potatoes.

Storing in a Root Cellar

🌿 *Best method*

Potatoes are easily stored in open boxes, crates, or bins in the warmer area of your root cellar (approximately 40°F) or any cool, dark room or outbuilding. Potatoes stored below 38°F decline in starch and increase in sugar, which destroys their keeping and cooking qualities.

Do not store potatoes in the same root cellar as apples, unless both products are in well-covered containers and the room is well ventilated.

store potatoes in crate

Drying Potatoes

① Wash and peel potatoes. Cut into ½-inch shoestring strips or ⅛-inch slices.

② Dry in a dehydrator at 120°F for 12 to 18 hours, turning pieces occasionally, until brittle and semitransparent. Or dry in a conventional oven at 120°F for 18 to 24 hours, turning occasionally and rotating trays once, until brittle.

③ Cool and package in airtight containers.

SUMMER SQUASH

SUMMER SQUASH IS BEST EATEN DRIED; try it as a snack with a dip, or chop and add directly to salads.

If you can't preserve right away, do not wash the squash. Store by one of the methods suggested in chapter 2.

tips ✲ Squash can be sliced ½ inch thick and tray-frozen, unblanched, to be breaded or flour-coated and fried. Do not defrost squash before frying.

✲ Squash to be frozen, dried, or pickled should be harvested when it is small and firm, and the seeds are underdeveloped. Zucchini is at its best when it is 6 to 10 inches long; yellow types, 5 to 7 inches long; and scallop types, about 4 to 5 inches in diameter. Squash grows fast and should not be allowed to remain on the vine past the time it reaches proper size.

✲ Zucchini can be grated and frozen for fruit breads, cookies, and muffins. When defrosting, squeeze the moisture out of squash before measuring and adding to recipe.

Drying Squash Chips

① Wash and cut into ½-inch slices; do not peel.

② Dry in a dehydrator at 120°F for 6 to 8 hours, turning once, until crisp. Or dry in a conventional oven at 120°F for 6 to 8 hours, until crisp.

③ Cool and package in airtight containers.

Freezing Unblanched Squash Slices
✏ *Best and quickest method for stir-frying*

① Wash. Drain. Pat dry.

② Trim ends. Slice no thicker than ¼ inch.

③ Pack in gallon-size freezer bags. Press out air. Seal. Freeze.

Note: Will retain good quality for 4 to 6 months.

> cooking tip ❖ **For best flavor and texture, cook frozen squash by stir-frying with pork drippings or butter and seasonings (garlic is great), for 2 minutes, or steam for 4 minutes.**

Freezing Squash in Boilable Bags
✏ *Excellent finished product*

① Wash squash. Drain. Pat dry. Trim ends. Slice in ¼-inch slices. Pack in boilable bags. Add butter and seasonings, if desired. Press out air. Seal bags.

② Blanch bags, four at a time, in boiling water for 5 minutes.

③ Cool bags in ice water. Pat bags dry. Freeze.

seal bags

TOMATOES

PICK TOMATOES WHEN THEY ARE FULLY RIPE and slightly soft to the touch. To be safely canned, tomatoes must be acidified with the addition of citric acid (¼ teaspoon per pint; ½ teaspoon per quart) or lemon juice (1 tablespoon per pint; 2 tablespoons per quart). Although you will find it faster to freeze tomatoes, canning produces a far superior end product.

Drying is a no-fuss way to preserve tomatoes and produces an excellent product, on par with expensive Italian sun-dried tomatoes.

> tip ❖ At the end of the harvest season, if you would like to hasten the ripening of tomatoes, place them in a single layer in large paper bags, tied loosely. The ethylene gases they release will help them to ripen rapidly and evenly.

Storing in a Root Cellar
🌱 *Best method*

cover with newspaper

Tomatoes that are good for eating fresh, although not as tasty as summer tomatoes, can be kept fairly well into the early winter if they are properly stored. Pick all large tomatoes just before a hard frost is predicted. Separate the green ones from those more advanced in color. Place the sorted tomatoes in a single layer in shallow boxes or on trays in a root cellar or cool garage. Cover with two to three layers of newspaper. Check frequently, and remove and eat tomatoes as they ripen. Remove any tomatoes that show signs of spoilage immediately. Green tomatoes stored this way will ripen in 4 to 6 weeks.

Freezing Whole, Unpeeled Tomatoes
🌱 *Quickest freezer method*

① Wash and core tomatoes. Set on cookie sheets and freeze.

② When tomatoes are frozen, pack in bags.

Preserving Vegetables

> **cooking tips** ❖ To use whole, unpeeled, frozen tomatoes, run them under tepid water for a few seconds to soften them slightly. Then peel and finish defrosting in a bowl. These tomatoes are best used in sauces, soups, and casseroles.
>
> ❖ To use whole frozen tomatoes in salads, run them under tepid water for a few seconds, peel, and set the tomatoes in a bowl for 30 minutes to soften slightly. Chop and serve in a bowl separate from the salad, to be added to the salad when served. After the tomatoes have been out of the freezer for an hour, they are too soft to use in salads.

Freezing Whole, Peeled Tomatoes

① Wash tomatoes. Heat water in a large kettle to boiling. Refill the sink with cold water. Drop tomatoes into boiling water a few at a time. Scald for 30 seconds. Remove to cold water. Lift from the water, peel, and core.

② Pack in rigid containers. Leave 1-inch headspace. Freeze.

> **tips** ❖ Always defrost tomatoes packaged in plastic bags in a bowl. Use the juice that separates out as well as the pulp, in order to keep all the nutrients.
>
> ❖ If you don't have a large hand-cranked strainer, you can make purées and juices with a blender or food mill, but you must cook the tomatoes to soften them before straining.

Freezing Strained Purée or Juice
🍃 *Best freezer product*

① Wash, core, and quarter tomatoes.

② Purée through a hand-cranked strainer.

③ Pack in rigid containers. Leave 1-inch headspace. Freeze.

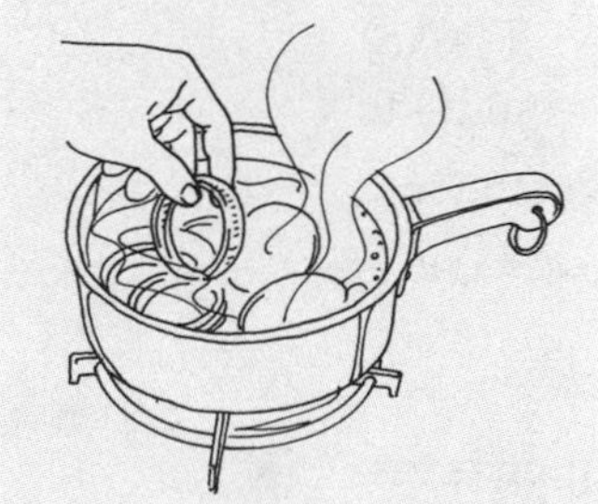

place lids in water

pour purée into jars

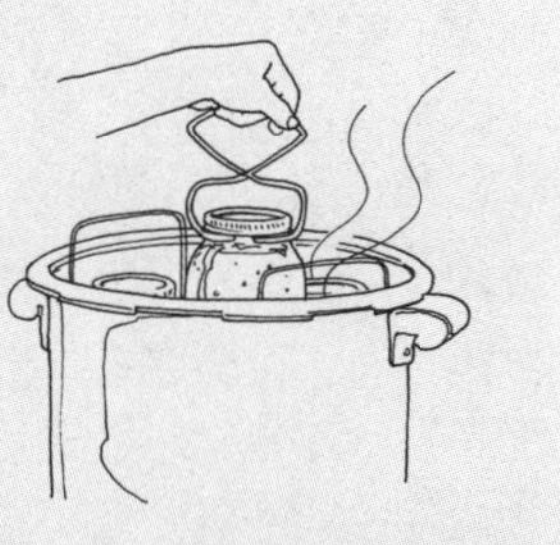

lower jar into canner

Canning Tomato Purée

Best finished product

① Wash, core, and quarter tomatoes.

② Purée in a hand-cranked strainer.

③ Heat purée to boiling. Simmer for 5 minutes.

④ While the purée is heating, preheat the water in the boiling-water-bath canner and jars. Place the jar lids and screw bands in water according to manufacturer's directions.

⑤ Pour the hot purée into the heated jars, leaving ½-inch headspace. Add citric acid (¼ teaspoon per pint, ½ teaspoon per quart) or lemon juice (1 tablespoon per pint, 2 tablespoons per quart). Add salt (½ teaspoon per pint, 1 teaspoon per quart), if desired.

⑥ Load the canner and process: pints for 35 minutes, quarts for 40 minutes.

tips

- **Freeze or can tomatoes whole or in a purée in the summer; make up sauces, soups chilis, ketchups, relishes, and chutneys when the woodstove is going in the winter.**
- **Tomato juice or purée made in a blender or strainer must be heated to boiling and simmered for 5 minutes to remove air; otherwise the jars will not seal properly.**

Canning Raw-Packed Whole Tomatoes
🐚 Best finished product

① Begin heating water in the blancher, boiling-water-bath canner, and teakettle. Wash tomatoes. Refill the sink or a large pan with cold water. Drop tomatoes in boiling water, a few at a time. Scald for 30 seconds. Remove to cold water. Lift tomatoes from the cold water. Peel and core tomatoes.

② Add citric acid (¼ teaspoon per pint, ½ teaspoon per quart) or lemon juice (1 tablespoon per pint, 2 tablespoons per quart) to each hot jar. Pack tomatoes in tightly, leaving ½-inch headspace. Add boiling water or juice to leave ½-inch headspace. Add salt (½ teaspoon per pint, 1 teaspoon per quart), if desired.

③ Load the canner and process pints for 45 minutes, quarts for 50 minutes.

Drying Tomato Slices
🐚 Excellent finished product

① Wash tomatoes, cut out cores, and slice ¼ inch thick.

② Dry in a dehydrator at 120°F for 8 to 10 hours, then turn slices and dry for another 6 to 8 hours, until crisp. Or dry in a conventional oven at 120°F for 18 to 24 hours, until crisp, turning slices and rotating trays once or twice. Or dry in the sun for 1 to 2 days, until brittle, taking the trays in at night.

③ Cool and package in airtight containers.

> tip ❖ For that imported Italian sun-dried tomato flavor, pour boiling water over dried tomato slices to partially rehydrate them. Drain. Pack in clean jars and cover with extra-virgin olive oil. Store in a cool place and use within a few months. As long as the tomatoes are completely covered with oil, they will not mold.

dry squash in sun

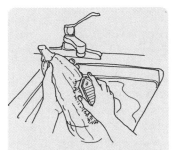

wash with bleach and water

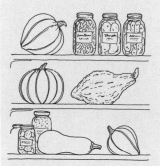

leave air space between squash

WINTER SQUASH AND PUMPKINS

SQUASH AND PUMPKINS FOR WINTER STORAGE should not be picked until they are fully mature and have attained the full color common to their type. Skins should be too hard to be pierced with your thumbnail. Leave at least 1 inch of stem on the fruit when you pick it.

Storing in a Root Cellar
Best and quickest method

① When harvesting squash and pumpkins, leave them in the sun or a warm room (65°F to 75°F) for 2 weeks to cure. This extra time will make rinds harder. Acorn squash should be stored without curing.

② Wash the vegetables with a solution of ½ cup chlorine bleach to 1 gallon of cold water. This mixture will prevent bacteria growth during storage.

③ Store in a dry, well-ventilated area at 50°F to 60°F. Leave space between fruit to allow good air circulation.

Preserving
Vegetables

93

tips ✻ Squash and pumpkins should keep well into mid-winter when any excess can be frozen or canned.

✻ Steam squash and pumpkins for freezing when the wood-stove is going in the winter.

Freezing Strained Squash in Boilable Bags

① Wash squash; cut in quarters or smaller. Steam until tender, 45 to 60 minutes.

② Scoop out seeds. Scoop out pulp into a hand-cranked strainer and purée (or mash with a potato masher).

③ Pack in 1-pint boilable freezer bags. Add butter and seasoning, if desired. Press out air. Seal bags.

④ Cool. Wipe dry. Freeze.

Note: Use an ice cream scoop to remove squash seeds and scoop pulp from rind.

> cooking tip ❋ **For best flavor and texture, reheat frozen squash in boilable bags for 20 minutes or in a double boiler or microwave until piping hot.**

mix vegetables in pan

chill vegetables in ice water

pack in rigid containers

MIXED VEGETABLES FOR SOUPS AND PURÉES

AT THE END OF THE HARVEST SEASON, you may find yourself with an abundance of vegetables that have gone past their prime. These vegetables could be composted or fed to the pigs, but freezing vegetables for sauces and soups is an even better way to make use of them.

Freezing Mixed Soup Vegetables
❧ *Best and quickest method*

① Wash 16 to 20 pounds of vegetables. Peel if necessary. Slice, dice, julienne, or chop coarsely.

② Mix the vegetables in a large pan. Add water to cover. Bring to a boil. Remove from the heat; drain.

③ Cool in an ice bath for 30 minutes. Drain.

④ Stir well. Pack in rigid containers. Leave 1-inch headspace. Seal. Freeze.

> tip ❖ To freeze purées, chop the vegetables and cook in a minimum of water until mushy tender. Do not add seasoning. Purée in a hand-cranked strainer, blender, food mill, or fine sieve. Cool quickly and pack in rigid containers; leave 1-inch headspace.

Preserving Vegetables

95

CHAPTER 5

Preserving Fruits

MOST OF THE TECHNIQUES THAT APPLY to preserving vegetables apply to preserving fruit. Cold storage works well for apples, grapes, pears, and citrus fruit. Tray-freezing is quick for berries. Apples, cherries, peaches, nectarines, pears, and plums can all be canned. Drying makes sense for fruit, too. Quick snacks of sliced dried fruits or fruit leathers are real kid-pleasers.

As with vegetables, fruits contain enzymes that affect their quality after harvest. With some fruits, natural sugars rapidly convert to starch after harvest; the challenge there is to get the fruit into the freezer or canner or dehydrator as soon as possible. With others, the challenge is to prevent the natural enzymes from causing the fruit to darken and discolor.

Antioxidants Prevent Discoloration

SOME FRUITS, ESPECIALLY APPLES, peaches, and pears, will discolor if left exposed to the air. The way to avoid this discoloration is to work quickly and in small batches, and to treat them with any of the following antioxidants:

✳ A commercial preparation such as Fruit-Fresh, according to label directions.

✳ One teaspoon or 3,000 mg ascorbic acid (vitamin C) to 1 gallon of water. Dip the fruit in as you go along. Or add ¼ teaspoon ascorbic acid per quart as you pack fruit into jars if you didn't soak them beforehand. Ascorbic acid in crystalline form can be obtained at drugstores.

✳ A solution of 5 tablespoons lemon juice to 1 gallon cold water. Slice fruit into solution before packing. Work quickly and drain thoroughly; do not leave fruit in water longer than 15 minutes.

Please note: Before you start freezing, drying, or canning, turn back to chapter 3 for a quick review of the basic techniques. Assembling all your equipment, setting up for a productive work flow, and ensuring the safety of your methods will help to save you time in the long run.

Sugar Syrups

FOR CANNING AND FREEZING MOST SLICED FRUITS, a sugar syrup is recommended. The sugar is not needed as a preservative, but it does help the fruit maintain a good texture and color. You can substitute honey or maple syrup for the sugar, sweetened or unsweetened fruit juice for the syrup, or plain water. I find that a light sugar syrup makes an excellent product; using unsweetened juices or water leaves the fruit mushy and flat-tasting.

Figure that you will need ½ to ¾ cup syrup or liquid for each pint of fruit, or 1 to 1½ cups syrup or liquid for each quart.

SUGAR SYRUPS FOR CANNING AND FREEZING A 7-QUART LOAD		
	Water or Fruit Juice	Sugar
Very light syrup	10½ cups	1¼ cups
Light syrup	9 cups	2¼ cups
Medium syrup	8¼ cups	3¾ cups
Heavy syrup	7¾ cups	5¼ cups

To make syrups, heat water and sugar together. Bring to a boil and stir to dissolve the sugar. Pour over raw fruits in jars for raw-packs. For hot-packs, bring water and sugar to a boil, add fruit, reheat to boiling, stir, and fill jars immediately.

At the end of each fruit entry, I have included instructions for making juice. Since quality fruit juices are readily available in the supermarket, you may not feel the necessity of making juice. However, I've found it worthwhile to make juice from homegrown fruits to use in jelly later in the year, when I am freed from gardening and other preserving tasks, so I included the information here. Juices can be frozen (never skimp on the headspace if you are using glass jars) or canned in a boiling-water bath. I can unsweetened juices as most of my juices end up as jelly, where the amount of sugar is specified by the recipe. If you are planning to drink the juice, you can sweeten with a sugar syrup or other sweetener before or after canning or freezing.

It is important to preserve most fruit as soon as possible after harvest. The sugars in ripe fruit begin to convert to starch immediately after harvest. Some fruits, such as pears and apples, are usually picked underripe; these should be put in cold storage as soon as possible but can be left at room temperature for a day or two if you are planning to preserve them by any other method. Fruits that are to be dried, in particular, should be fully ripe.

APPLES

APPLES STORE WELL IN A ROOT CELLAR and dry beautifully. Applesauce is a staple in most households, and homemade apple-sauce is far superior to commercial products. Homemade applesauce can be canned or frozen. Finally, apples make great jams and jellies (for recipes, see chapter 8). The natural pectin in apples makes them easy to handle in jams and jellies — they can even be combined with other low-pectin fruits to make a firmer jelly.

Storing in a Root Cellar
Best and quickest method

① Place a large plastic bag in a cardboard box; add 2 to 4 inches of fresh sawdust (2 inches for storage areas that will remain above freezing).

② Add a single layer of apples, leaving a 2-inch space all around the side of the layer to be filled with sawdust. Cover with a 1-inch layer of sawdust. Continue to layer the apples until the box is full. Finish with a 2- to 4-inch layer of sawdust.

③ Fold over the top of the bag and close the box. Store in the coldest area of the root cellar or in an unheated area, such as a garage. Do not store near potatoes.

④ Use by the end of the winter.

Drying Apple Slices
Excellent finished product

① Wash and core apples; peeling is optional. Cut in wedges, then in ¼-inch slices; or cut in ¼-inch crosswise rings.

② Pretreat if drying in the sun. Pretreating is optional with oven-drying and not necessary at all if you work quickly and slice directly onto dehydrator trays. To pretreat, dip slices in ascorbic

acid or commerical fruit dip (page 43), then soak for 1 hour in diluted lemon juice (¼ cup lemon juice to 4 cups water) or full-strength pineapple juice.

③ Dry in a dehydrator or in a conventional oven at 115°F for 6 to 8 hours, stirring or turning the fruit once. After the first 6 hours, test for dryness every 2 hours, until no moisture remains in the center when a slice is bitten. Or dry in the sun for 2 to 3 days, until leathery and chewy, with no sign of crispness in the centers. Take trays inside at night.

④ Cool and package in airtight containers.

Freezing Apple Slices with Sugar Syrup

① Prepare medium syrup (page 98) and set aside. Wash, peel, core, and slice apples. Pretreat with an antioxidant (page 97), if desired.

② Pack slices in a rigid container and cover with syrup, allowing ½-inch headspace for pints and 1 inch for quarts.

③ Seal and freeze.

Freezing Apple Slices with Sugar
Good for use in pies and other baked goods

① Wash, peel, core, and slice apples. Pretreat with an antioxidant (page 97), if desired.

② Sprinkle ¼ cup sugar over each quart of apples; toss to coat well. Allow to stand until juice is drawn out and sugar is dissolved. Pack slices in a rigid container and cover with the juices, allowing ½-inch headspace for pints and 1 inch for quarts.

③ Seal and freeze.

> **tip** ✣ An easy way to freeze apples for pies is to prepare the pie filling as you would if you were baking right away. Freeze the filling in a pie tin. When frozen, slip out of the pie tin, wrap in freezer paper, and return to the freezer. When you are ready to bake, slip the frozen apples into a prepared pie shell and bake. Thawing first is not necessary.

Freezing Applesauce
✍ Quickest method for applesauce

① Wash and quarter apples. Don't peel. Put in heavy-bottomed kettle with just enough water to keep the apples from scorching. Cover and cook until soft, stirring occasionally and adding water, 1 tablespoon at a time if needed.

② Pass through a hand-cranked strainer or food mill. Add sweetener to taste, if desired.

③ Cool prepared applesauce and pack into rigid containers, leaving ½-inch headspace for pints, 1 inch for quarts.

> **tip** ✣ Thawing applesauce takes some time, unless you have a microwave oven. You may find it more convenient to can the applesauce than to freeze it.

Preserving
Fruits

101

Making Apple Fruit Leather
✍ Excellent finished product

① Core and cut up four medium apples, without peeling. Add ½ cup water and cook over medium heat for 15 to 20 minutes, or until tender. Force through a sieve or colander and stir in ¼ cup honey.

② Line a drying tray with plastic wrap (or use the fruit leather sheet that came with your dehydrator). Spread the purée ½-inch thick on the trays.

③ Dry in a dehydrator at 120°F for 6 to 8 hours, or until leather can be pulled easily from the plastic. Invert, pull off plastic, and continue drying for another 4 to 6 hours. Dry in the oven at 120°F for 6 to 8 hours, or until leather can be pulled easily from the plastic. Invert, pull off plastic, and continue drying for another 6 to 8 hours. Dry in the sun for 1 day, or until leather can be pulled easily from the plastic. Invert, pull off plastic, and dry for 1 more day.

④ To store, roll up in waxed paper or plastic wrap, close and twist ends, and store in the refrigerator for up to 6 weeks.

Canning Applesauce
🡒 Excellent finished product

Even though it takes time to make applesauce, it yields such a wonderful finished product that you may find it well worth your time. Figure that 21 pounds of apples will yield a canner load of 7 quarts of applesauce.

① Wash and quarter apples. Don't peel. Put in a heavy-bottomed kettle filled with 2 inches of water. Cover and cook until soft, stirring occasionally to prevent scorching. Begin preheating water in the canner and teakettle and preparing jars and lids.

② Pass softened apples through a hand-cranked strainer or food mill. Add sweetener to taste, if desired. Reheat sauce to boiling.

③ Pack hot applesauce in hot, clean jars, leaving ½-inch headspace. Process pints for 15 minutes, quarts for 20 minutes.

Making Apple Juice (Frozen or Canned)

① Sterilize jars for canning or prepare containers for freezing. Begin heating water in the canner, if using.

② Select a variety of apples for best flavor. Wash and quarter; do not peel or core. Place in a saucepan and cover with boiling water. Heat and simmer until soft, 25 to 30 minutes.

③ Press through a damp jelly bag or double layers of cheesecloth. Strain again through cheesecloth or coffee filter paper.

④ To freeze, pour into freezer containers, leaving 1½-inch headspace. Freeze.

⑤ To can, reheat juice, stirring occasionally, to boiling. Pour into hot jars, leaving ¼-inch headspace. Process pints or quarts for 5 minutes.

APRICOTS

DRIED APRICOTS ARE A REAL TREAT, and with apricot season so brief, it may be that more apricots are consumed dried than fresh or canned. Select perfectly ripe apricots for preserving. The fruit should not be mushy, but green fruit does not dry well and will not have full flavor after it is canned or frozen.

Drying Apricot Halves
Best and quickest method

① Peel apricots by dipping in boiling water for 1 minute, then in ice water for 1 minute. Skins will slip off easily. Cut in half, removing the pits.

② Dip in commercial fruit dip or ascorbic acid solution (page 43).

③ Dry in a dehydrator at 115°F for 36 to 48 hours, stirring or turning the fruit occasionally and rotating trays, until the fruit is leathery. Dry in a conventional oven at 115°F for 2 to 3 days, stirring or turning the fruit occasionally and rotating trays, until the fruit is leathery. Or dry in the sun for 4 or more days, until leathery. Take trays inside at night.

④ Cool and package in airtight containers.

> **tip** ❖ To speed drying, spread halves, pit side up, on trays and dry until they begin to wrinkle. Turn halves over and flatten with your hand, a spatula, or a block of wood.

Freezing Apricot Halves with Sugar Syrup

① Prepare medium syrup (page 98). Add ¾ teaspoon of crystalline ascorbic acid to each quart of syrup, and set aside. Dip apricots in boiling water for 1 minute, then in ice water for 1 minute. Peel, cut in half, and remove pits.

② Pack in a rigid container and cover with syrup, allowing ½-inch headspace for pints and 1 inch for quarts.

③ Seal and freeze.

Freezing Apricot Halves with Sugar

① Dip apricots in boiling water for 1 minute, then in ice water for 1 minute. Peel, cut in half, and remove pits.

② Sprinkle ¼ teaspoon ascorbic acid dissolved in ¼ cup water over each quart of apricots. Mix ½ cup of sugar with each quart of apricots, toss to coat well. Allow to stand until juice is drawn out and sugar is dissolved.

③ Pack in a rigid container, allowing ½-inch headspace for pints and quarts.

④ Seal and freeze.

Making Apricot Fruit Leather

① Dip ripe apricots in boiling water for 1 minute, then in ice water. Slip off skins and cut in half. Remove pits and process fruit in a blender until puréed.

② Line a drying tray with plastic wrap (or use the fruit leather sheet that came with your dehydrator). Spread the purée ½ inch thick on the trays.

③ Dry in a dehydrator at 120°F for 6 to 8 hours, or until leather can be pulled easily from the plastic. Invert, pull off plastic, and continue drying for another 4 to 6 hours. Dry in a conventional oven at 120°F for 6 to 8 hours or until leather can be pulled easily from the plastic. Invert, pull off plastic, and continue drying for another 6 to 8 hours. Dry in the sun for 1 day, or until leather can be pulled easily from the plastic. Invert, pull off plastic, and dry for 1 more day.

④ To store, roll in waxed paper or plastic wrap, close and twist ends, and store in the refrigerator for up to 6 weeks.

Raw-Pack Canning Apricot Halves
Excellent finished product

Figure that 16 pounds of fruit will yield 7 quarts. Select firm apricots that are ready for eating.

① Dip in boiling water for 1 minute, then in ice water. Slip off skins, cut in half, and remove pits. Place in ascorbic acid solution (see page 43). Prepare very light, light, or medium syrup (page 98), if using.

② Begin preheating water in the canner and teakettle. Prepare jars and lids for hot-pack. Heat syrup or juice.

③ Drain fruit and pack into hot jars, leaving ½-inch headspace. Pack fruit cut-side down. Fill with hot liquid, leaving ½-inch headspace.

④ Process pints for 25 minutes, quarts for 30 minutes.

BLUEBERRIES

Tray-Freezing Whole Berries
Best and quickest method

① Wash berries and drain on towels. Pat dry with another towel.

② Place dry berries on waxed-paper-lined cookie sheets and freeze until solid.

③ Within 24 hours, package loosely in plastic bags and return to freezer.

Freezing Blueberries in Sugar
Excellent finished product

① Wash berries and drain on towels. Pat dry with another towel.

② Add ½ cup of sugar to each quart of berries and mix well.

③ Pack into containers, leaving ½-inch headspace.

④ Seal and freeze.

> tip ❖ Berries packed with sugar retain their texture better than berries frozen unsweetened. The best way to preserve berries for use in pies is with sugar.

Drying Whole Berries

① Dip in boiling water for 30 seconds to split the skins.

② Dry the berries in a dehydrator at 115°F for 12 to 24 hours, stirring occasionally and rotating trays, until the fruit is hard but still chewy. Dry in an oven at 115°F for 18 to 36 hours, stirring occasionally and rotating trays, until the fruit is hard but still chewy. Or dry in the sun for 2 to 4 days, until hard but chewy. Take trays inside at night.

③ Cool and package in airtight containers.

> **tips** ❖ For extra flavor, blueberries can be dipped in a honey solution before drying. Dissolve 1 cup sugar in 3 cups hot water. Cool to lukewarm and stir in 1 cup honey. Dip berries in solution and remove with a slotted spoon. Drain well before drying.
>
> ❖ Honey-dipped or plain, dried berries and cherries are delicious eaten as a confection. They can be directly added to breakfast cereals and muffin and cake batters.

CHERRIES

Freezing Tart Cherries in Sugar
🍃 *Best method*

① Wash cherries, stem, and pit, using a cherry pitter or sharp paring knife.

② Add ¾ cup of sugar to each quart of cherries and mix well.

③ Pack into containers, leaving ½-inch headspace.

④ Seal and freeze.

Freezing Sweet Cherries in Sugar Syrup

① Prepare heavy syrup (page 98) and set aside. Wash and pit cherries.

② Pack cherries in a rigid container and cover with syrup, allowing ½-inch headspace for pints and 1 inch for quarts.

③ Seal and freeze.

Drying Whole Cherries
Quickest method

① Wash and pit fully ripe sweet or tart cherries. Drain well.

② Dry untreated cherries in a dehydrator at 115°F for 24 hours, stirring occasionally and rotating trays, until the fruit is chewy but dry. Dry in a conventional oven at 115°F for 18 to 36 hours, stirring occasionally and rotating trays, until the cherries are dry but still chewy. Or dry in the sun for 4 to 5 days, until chewy but dry. Take trays inside at night.

③ Cool and package in airtight containers.

> **tip ❖ Dried sweet or tart cherries are a delicious alternative to raisins and can be used in exactly the same ways.**

Making Cherry Fruit Leather

① Pit 2 cups tart cherries. Combine in a blender with ½ cup sugar. Process until sugar is dissolved and fruit is puréed.

② Line a drying tray with plastic wrap (or use the fruit leather sheet that came with your dehydrator). Spread the purée ½-inch thick on the trays.

③ Dry in a dehydrator at 120°F for 6 to 8 hours, or until leather can be pulled easily from the plastic. Invert, pull off plastic, and continue drying for another 4 to 6 hours. Dry in a conventional oven at 120°F for 6 to 8 hours or until leather can be pulled easily from the plastic. Invert, pull off plastic, and continue drying for another 6 to 8 hours. Dry in the sun for 1 day, or until leather can be pulled easily from the plastic. Invert, pull off plastic, and dry for 1 more day.

④ To store, roll in waxed paper or plastic wrap, close and twist ends, and store in the refrigerator for up to 6 weeks.

Raw-Pack Canning Sweet or Sour Cherries
❧ Excellent finished product

Figure that 17½ pounds of fruit will yield 7 quarts. Select bright, uniformly colored cherries.

① Stem and wash cherries. Pit with a cherry pitter or paring knife.

② Begin preheating water in the canner and teakettle. Prepare jars and lids according to the manufacturer's recommendations.

③ Prepare syrup of any weight (page 98), if using, and keep warm. Or heat water, apple juice, or white grape juice to boiling and keep warm.

④ Add ½ cup hot syrup, juice, or water to each jar. Fill with cherries, shaking down gently as you fill. Add more hot liquid, leaving ½-inch headspace.

⑤ Process pints or quarts for 25 minutes.

Preserving
Fruits

109

CRANBERRIES

ALTHOUGH CRANBERRIES ARE NOT A GARDENER'S DELIGHT, they are a wonderful fruit that is available in the supermarkets for only a few short months each year. Freezing is by far the easiest method of preserving these underutilized berries, but drying is also good, if only because dried cranberries make such a delightful alternative to raisins in baked goods.

Freezing Whole Cranberries
❧ *Best and quickest method*

Simply place the cranberries, still in their original packaging, in the freezer. No washing or processing is necessary.

Drying Whole Cranberries

① Dip in boiling water for 30 seconds to split skins. Drain well.

② Dry untreated berries in a dehydrator at 115°F for 12 to 24 hours, stirring occasionally and rotating trays, until the fruit is hard but still chewy. Dry in a conventional oven at 115°F for 18 to 36 hours, stirring occasionally and rotating trays, until fruit is hard but still chewy. Or dry in the sun for 2 to 4 days, until hard but chewy. Take trays inside at night.

③ Cool and package in airtight containers.

> tip ✿ For extra flavor, cranberries can be dipped in a honey solution before drying. Dissolve 1 cup sugar in 3 cups hot water. Cool to lukewarm and stir in 1 cup honey. Dip berries in solution and remove with a slotted spoon. Drain well before drying.

Canning Cranberry Sauce
Excellent finished product

① Begin preheating water in the canner and teakettle. Prepare jars and lids.

② Combine 8 cups fresh or frozen cranberries with 2 cups water in a saucepan. Cook until berries are soft. Add 4 cups sugar and boil for 3 minutes.

③ Pack into hot jars, leaving ½-inch headspace.

④ Process pints and quarts for 15 minutes.

GRAPES

Storing in a Root Cellar
Best and quickest method

① Place a large plastic bag in a cardboard box; add 2 to 4 inches of fresh sawdust (2 inches for storage areas that will remain above freezing).

Preserving
Fruits

111

② Add a single layer of grapes, leaving a 2-inch space all around the side of the layer to be filled with sawdust. Cover with a 1-inch layer of sawdust. Continue to layer the grapes until the box is full. Finish with a 2- to 4-inch layer of sawdust.

③ Fold over the top of the bag and close the box. Store in the coldest area of the root cellar or in an unheated area, such as a garage.

④ Use within 1 to 2 months.

Making Raisins

① Leave grapes whole, or cut in half. Seed as needed. Whole seedless grapes should be dipped in boiling water for 30 seconds to split skins. Drain well.

② Dry grapes in a dehydrator at 115°F for 24 to 48 hours, stirring occasionally and rotating trays, until the fruit is dry to the center. Dry in a conventional oven at 115°F for 48 to 72 hours, stirring occasionally and rotating trays, until wrinkled and dry to the center. Or dry in the sun for 3 to 5 days, until wrinkled and dry to the center. Take trays inside at night.

③ Cool and package in airtight containers.

Making Grape Juice
Excellent finished product

① Wash and stem grapes. Place in a saucepan and cover with boiling water. Heat and simmer until skins are soft. Strain through a damp jelly bag or double layers of cheesecloth. Refrigerate juice for 24 to 48 hours. Without mixing the juice, carefully pour off the clear liquid, and discard any sediment in the bottom of the container.

② Begin heating water in the teakettle and canner, if using. Sterilize jars for canning or prepare containers for freezing.

③ To freeze, pour into freezer containers, leaving 1½ inches headspace.

④ To can, pour into sterilized, hot jars, leaving ¼-inch headspace. Process pints or quarts for 5 minutes.

NECTARINES AND PEACHES

Freezing Nectarines and Peaches in Sugar
🖎 *Best and quickest method*

① Peel ripe peaches by briefly dipping into boiling water, then in ice water. Slip off the skins, cut in half, and remove pits. Nectarines do not need peeling.

② Add ⅔ cup of sugar to each quart of fruit and mix well.

③ Pack into containers, leaving 1-inch headspace.

④ Seal and freeze.

Freezing Nectarines and Peaches in Sugar Syrup
🖎 *Best and quickest method*

① Prepare medium syrup (page 98) and set aside. To peel, briefly dip peaches in boiling water, then in ice water. Slip off skins, slice in half, and remove pits. Nectarines do not require peeling.

② Pack in a rigid container and cover with syrup, allowing ½-inch headspace for pints and 1 inch for quarts.

③ Seal and freeze.

Preserving
Fruits

113

Drying Nectarine and Peach Halves

① Peel peaches by dipping in boiling water for 1 minute, then in cold water for 1 minute. Skins will slip off easily. Cut in half, removing the pits. Nectarines do not need peeling.

② Dip in commercial fruit dip or ascorbic acid solution (page 98).

③ Dry in a dehydrator at 115°F for 24 to 36 hours, stirring or turning the fruit occasionally and rotating trays, until the fruit is leathery with no hint of moisture when bitten. Dry in a conventional oven at

115°F for 36 to 48 hours, stirring or turning the fruit occasionally and rotating trays, until the fruit is leathery with no hint of moisture when bitten. Or dry in the sun for 4 to 6 days, until leathery and almost stiff, with no hint of moisture in the center. Take trays inside at night.

④ Cool and package in airtight containers.

> **tip** ❖ To speed drying, spread halves, pit side up, on trays and dry until they begin to wrinkle. Turn halves over and flatten with your hand, a spatula, or a block of wood.

Making Nectarine and Peach Fruit Leather

① Select ripe or slightly overripe fruit. Peel and cut in halves. Remove pits and purée in blender.

② Line a drying tray with plastic wrap (or use the fruit leather sheet that came with your dehydrator). Spread the purée ½ inch thick on the trays.

③ Dry in a dehydrator at 120°F for 6 to 8 hours, or until leather can be pulled easily from the plastic. Invert, pull off plastic, and continue drying for another 4 to 6 hours. Dry in a conventional oven at 120°F for 6 to 8 hours or until leather can be pulled easily from the plastic. Invert, pull off plastic, and continue drying for another 6 to 8 hours. Dry in the sun for 1 day, or until leather can be pulled easily from the plastic. Invert, pull off plastic, and dry for 1 more day.

④ To store, roll in waxed paper or plastic wrap, close and twist ends, and store in the refrigerator for up to 6 weeks.

Canning Nectarine and Peach Halves
Excellent finished product

Figure that 17½ pounds of fruit will yield 7 quarts. Select ripe, mature fruit that is ready for eating.

① Briefly dip peaches in boiling water, then in ice water. Slip off skins, cut in half, and remove pits. Nectarines do not need peeling. Place in ascorbic acid solution (see page 43). Prepare very light, light, or medium syrup (page 98), if using.

② Begin preheating water in the canner and teakettle. Prepare jars and lids.

③ Drain fruit and pack cut-side down in jars, leaving ½-inch headspace.

④ Fill jars with hot syrup, water, or fruit juice, leaving ½-inch headspace.

⑤ Process pints for 25 minutes, quarts for 30.

PEARS

Storing in a Root Cellar
Best and quickest method

① Place a large plastic bag in a cardboard box; add 2 to 4 inches of fresh sawdust (2 inches for storage areas that will remain above freezing).

② Add a single layer of slightly immature pears, leaving a 2-inch space all around the side of the layer to be filled with sawdust. Cover with a 1-inch layer of sawdust. Continue to layer the pears until the box is full. Finish with a 2- to 4-inch layer of sawdust.

③ Fold over the top of the bag and close the box. Store in the coldest area of the root cellar or in an unheated area, such as a garage.

④ Use by the end of winter.

Freezing Pears in Sugar Syrup

① Prepare a syrup by mixing 3 cups sugar to 4 cups water. Bring to a boil, stirring to dissolve sugar, then let cool.

② Wash, peel, and core pears. Place in an antioxidant bath (page 97).

③ Drain pears and blanch for 2 minutes in boiling water to cover. Cool in ice water immediately. Drain. Pack in a rigid container and cover with syrup, allowing ½-inch headspace for pints and 1 inch for quarts.

④ Seal and freeze.

Hot-Pack Canning Pear Halves
Excellent finished product

Figure that 16 pounds of fruit will yield 7 quarts. Select firm pears that are ready for eating, and choose varieties other than Asian pears, which are too low-acid for this method.

① Begin preheating water in the canner and teakettle. Prepare jars and lids.

② Wash and peel pears. Cut in half and core pears (a melon baller works well). Place in ascorbic acid solution (see page 43). Prepare very light, light, or medium syrup (page 98), if using.

③ Drain pears and combine in a large saucepan with syrup or water, apple juice, or white grape juice. Bring to a boil and boil for 5 minutes.

④ Fill hot jars with hot fruit, cut-side down, and cooking liquid, leaving ½-inch headspace. Place halves in layers.

⑤ Process pints for 20 minutes, quarts for 25 minutes.

PINEAPPLES

Freezing Unsweetened Pineapple Slices
Quickest method

① Wash, peel, core, and slice pineapple. Pack into containers, leaving ½-inch headspace.

② Seal and freeze.

Freezing Pineapple Slices in Sugar Syrup
Excellent finished product

① Prepare a light syrup (page 98) made with water or pineapple juice and set aside. Wash, peel, core, and slice pineapple.

② Pack slices in a rigid container and cover with syrup, allowing ½-inch headspace for pints and 1 inch for quarts.

③ Seal and freeze.

Drying Pineapple Slices

① Wash, peel, and core pineapple; cut into 1-inch slices. No pre-treatment is necessary, but dipping in a honey solution as with blueberries (see page 107) is highly recommended.

② Dry in a dehydrator at 115°F for 24 to 36 hours, stirring or turning the fruit occasionally and rotating trays, until the fruit is chewy and dried through. Dry in a conventional oven at 115°F for 36 to 48 hours, stirring or turning the fruit occasionally and rotating trays, until the fruit is chewy and dried through. Or dry in the sun for 4 to 5 days, until the fruit is chewy and dried through. Take trays inside at night.

③ Cool and package in airtight containers.

Hot-Pack Canning Pineapple Slices
🪶 *Excellent finished product*

① Begin preheating water in the canner and teakettle. Prepare jars and lids for hot-pack.

② Peel and remove eyes and tough fibers from pineapple. Slice and core.

③ Prepare very light, light, or medium syrup (page 98), if using.

④ Combine pineapple in a large saucepan with syrup, water, or pineapple juice. Bring to a boil, reduce heat, and simmer for 10 minutes.

⑤ Fill jars with hot fruit and cooking liquid, leaving ½-inch headspace.

⑥ Process pints for 15 minutes, quarts for 20 minutes.

PLUMS

Drying Whole Prunes
🪶 *Best and quickest method*

① Wash and dip plums in boiling water for 1 minute to crack skins.

② Dry in a dehydrator at 115°F for 18 to 24 hours, turning the fruit and rotating the trays every few hours, until the fruit is chewy but dry in the center. Dry in a conventional oven at 115°F for 24 to 36 hours, stirring or turning the fruit occasionally and rotating trays, until the fruit is chewy but dry in the center. Or dry in the sun for 36 to 48 hours, until the fruit is chewy but dry in the center. Take trays inside at night.

③ Cool and package in airtight containers.

Raw-Pack Canning Plums

① Begin preheating water in the canner and teakettle. Prepare jars and lids.

② Prick skins on 2 sides of plums to prevent splitting. Freestone plums can be halved and pitted, if desired. Prepare very light, light, or medium syrup (page 98), if using.

③ Fill jars with fruit and hot water, syrup, or juice, leaving ½-inch headspace.

④ Process pints for 20 minutes, quarts for 25 minutes.

RASPBERRIES

Tray-Freezing Whole Berries
🐾 *Best and quickest method*

① Wash berries and drain on towels. Pat dry with another towel.

② Place dry berries on waxed-paper-lined cookie sheets and freeze until solid.

③ Within 24 hours, package loosely in plastic bags and return to freezer.

Freezing Berries in Sugar
✎ *Excellent finished product*

① Wash berries and drain on towels. Pat dry with another towel.

② Add ½ cup of sugar to each quart of berries and mix well.

③ Pack into containers, leaving ½-inch headspace.

④ Seal and freeze.

> **tip** ❖ Berries packed with sugar retain their texture better than berries frozen unsweetened. The best way to preserve berries for use in pies is with sugar.

RHUBARB

AS SOON AS THE STALKS ARE as thick as your thumb, it is time to harvest rhubarb. Since both green and red varieties are common, don't use color as an indicator of readiness. To harvest, twist (don't cut) the outside stalks. Be sure to cut out the seedpods as they form in the center of the plant to prolong the harvest.

Since rhubarb is always eaten stewed or baked in a pie or cooked in a jam — preferably with plenty of sweetener — texture is less of a concern here than it is with most fruits. Frozen rhubarb can be defrosted and made into jam at a later date.

Freezing Unsweetened Rhubarb
✎ *Best and quickest method*

① Wash and trim off both ends of each stalk. Cut into 1-inch pieces. (The leaves contain oxalic acid, which is poisonous, so dispose of them in a place that is not within reach of children.)

② Pack into containers, leaving ½-inch headspace.

③ Seal and freeze.

Canning Sweetened Rhubarb
⁊ Excellent finished product

① Wash and trim off both ends of each stalk. Cut into 1-inch pieces. (The leaves contain oxalic acid, which is poisonous, so dispose of them in a place that is not within reach of children.)

② Add ½ cup sugar to each quart of sliced fruit. Let stand for several hours to draw out the juice.

③ Begin heating water in the canner and teakettle. Prepare jars and lids.

④ Boil the rhubarb for 1 minute.

⑤ Pack into clean, hot jars, leaving ½-inch headspace. Cover with hot juice, leaving ½-inch headspace. Process pints and quarts for 15 minutes.

STRAWBERRIES

Tray-Freezing Whole Berries
⁊ Quickest method

① Wash berries and drain on towels. Hull. Pat dry with another towel.

② Place dry berries on waxed-paper-lined cookie sheets and freeze until solid.

③ Within 24 hours, package loosely in plastic bags and return to the freezer.

Freezing Berries in Sugar

Excellent finished product

① Wash berries and drain on towels. Hull. Pat dry with another towel.

② Add ¾ cup of sugar to each quart of berries and mix well.

③ Pack into containers, leaving ½-inch headspace.

④ Seal and freeze.

tips ✲ **Berries packed with sugar retain their texture better than berries frozen unsweetened. Sweetened frozen strawberries can be thawed and served as a topping for pancakes, shortcake, or ice cream. Tray-frozen berries are best served semi-thawed so they retain their shape.**

✲ **Frozen fruit can be easily defrosted in a microwave. Set the microwave on DEFROST (30% power) and defrost 1-pint containers for 5 to 6 minutes and 1-quart containers for 9 to 10 minutes.**

CHAPTER 6

Preserving Herbs

THE MOST COMMON WAY to preserve herbs is to dry them. However, many herbs can be frozen, with the end product closer to fresh than dried. Frozen herbs, however, appear limp and are sometimes discolored, so they will not be suitable to use as garnishes or with most raw foods. However, frozen herbs are excellent in cooked dishes.

Herbs can also be preserved in pesto or other herb pastes, which freeze beautifully, or used to make teas, vinegars, and jellies. In this chapter, I start with drying and freezing herbs, and then give methods and recipes for various herbal products.

Drying Herbs: Fast and Convenient

PICK LEAVES AND FLOWERS FOR DRYING when the flower buds are about half open. If seeds are being harvested, they should be collected when the seed heads are turning brown. Pick before noon, as soon as the sun has dried off the dew. Use pruning shears to harvest, leaving about 4 inches of stem on annual herbs and about two-thirds of the stem on perennial herbs to permit further growth.

Wash herbs under running water or spray them, inspecting the leaves for dirt and insects as you do. Shake to remove moisture and pat dry.

The flavor of most dried herbs is much more pronounced than fresh herbs, so it is important to use very small amounts in cooking. A few herbs, including parsley, cilantro, and chives, lose flavor when dried and are far superior fresh or frozen.

Hang-Drying Herbs
❧ Best and quickest method

Hang-drying is definitely the fastest, easiest, and most popular way to preserve herbs. Just tie the freshly picked herbs together in small bunches and hang them upside down in a warm, dark, airy place. Some people place the herb bundles in paper bags with air holes punched in them to reduce the exposure to light and dust, but this isn't necessary if you are drying in a dark, airy attic.

The herbs should be dry in about 2 weeks — or when they crumble to the touch. Don't forget about them; allowing them to hang for too long reduces their quality.

Strip the leaves, crumble, and store in small glass jars. Keep in a cool, dry, dark place.

Dehydrator Drying

Be sure to dry only one type of herb at a time. Arrange herbs in a thin layer on dehydrator trays. Dry according to the times listed for each individual herb on pages 131 to 134, from 4 to 18 hours depending on the fleshiness of the leaves. Crumble and store in small glass jars. Keep in a cool, dry, dark place.

Oven-Drying Herbs

To keep flavors from mingling, dry only one type of herb at a time. Heat your oven to 200°F. Turn off the heat. Place a rack of herb leaves in the oven and leave for 6 to 8 hours or overnight. Or dry according to the directions given for each individual herb on pages 131 to 134.

Crumble and store in small glass jars. Keep in a cool, dry, dark place.

Freezing Herbs

SOME OF THE THICK, LEAFY HERBS, such as parsley and basil, can be frozen. Frozen herbs have the same pungency as fresh herbs, though they lack the crisp, fresh texture. Some herbs, like chives and cilantro, are better frozen than dried.

Freezing Herbs in Bags
Best and quickest method

To freeze herbs, gently wash freshly picked herbs, if necessary. Blot dry. Strip the leaves off the stalks and chop or leave whole. Pack into bags or containers, seal, and freeze.

Freezing Herb Pastes

A convenient way to preserve herbs is chopped and blended with enough oil to make a paste. This paste can be stored in the refrigerator for up to 1 month or frozen for up to 6 months. Herb pastes can be made into pesto — the traditional Italian herb paste made with basil, olive oil, parmesan cheese, and pine nuts — to dress pasta or add flavor to soups, stews, or salad dressings. A recipe for Pesto Pasta is found on page 206.

① Coarsely chop 2 cups fresh herb leaves in a food processor.

② Slowly drizzle in ⅓ cup high-quality olive or other salad oil while the motor is still running.

③ For immediate use, pack the herb paste in small jars; remove any air bubbles by running a knife through the mixture. Cover the top of the mixture with more oil to seal out any air, and refrigerate. For long-term storage, pack in jars, seal with oil, and freeze.

To have small quantities readily available for adding to a dish, drop by tablespoons onto waxed-paper-lined cookie sheets. Cover with plastic wrap and freeze. When frozen solid, place frozen mounds in a plastic bag, seal, and return to freezer.

> **tip** ✿ Pesto is traditionally made with basil, but other herbs such as chervil, cilantro, dill, fennel, marjoram, mint, parsley, rosemary, sage, savory, and tarragon also make delicious pastes.

Freezing Herbs in Ice Cubes
Good product for soups and stews

Wash and dry the herbs. Chop and spoon into an ice cube tray. Pour water over them and freeze. Pop them out of the tray and into the cooking pot as needed.

Herbal Products

THE HARVEST SEASON FOR HERBS extends throughout the summer. Somehow it always seems like there's enough time to make teas and vinegars, perhaps because they are usually made in small quantities. Also, you can make teas and vinegars with dried herbs, so even if the harvest season finds you flat out with gardening and preserving chores, you will probably be able to find some time during the year for making herb teas, vinegars, and jellies.

Herb Teas

Herb teas made from the dried leaves of herbs can be soothing or invigorating, spicy or mellow, good for serving hot or cold. It all depends on which herbs you select. There are no rules for combining herbs. You will have to experiment until you find a mix you like best.

Herb teas are usually steeped in hot water but not boiled. Simply place 1 teaspoon of dried herbs (or 1 tablespoon fresh herbs) into a tea strainer. Put this in a teacup and pour boiling water over it. Allow to steep for 5 to 7 minutes. Sweeten with honey or sugar, if desired.

Preserving
Herbs

127

FAVORITE HERBS FOR TEA		
Chamomile	Lemongrass	Mint
Lemon balm	Lemon verbena	Rose hips

Herb Vinegars

Herb-flavored vinegars add zing to a salad and provide a wonderful way to preserve the sprightly flavor of fresh herbs. Plus, they are very easy to make.

Select any herb, or combination of herbs, that you like. Wine vinegar is recommended as a base, as cider and white vinegars are so strongly flavored, they easily overpower the delicate herb flavor. As a general rule, white wine vinegar is used when color is important, such as with chive blossoms or opal basil, and red wine vinegar is used for strong flavors, such as basil, oregano, and garlic.

To make herb vinegar, follow these steps:

① Sanitize the fresh herbs by briefly dipping them in a solution of 1 teaspoon household bleach and 6 cups of water. Rinse the herbs well and pat them dry. Place 1 cup of the prepared herbs in a sterilized quart jar. Pour 3 to 3½ cups vinegar heated to just below boiling (190°F) over the herbs.

② Seal the jar and place in a cool, dark spot for 3 to 5 weeks. Shake the mixture every few days. Taste. If the mixture is too herbal, dilute with more vinegar. If the mixture isn't flavorful enough, repeat the procedure with fresh herbs.

③ Strain through a plastic (not metal) colander to remove the herbs. Then strain through paper coffee filters until the vinegar is crystal clear.

④ Pour the vinegar into hot, sterilized, dry jars. Add a sprig or two of fresh, sanitized herbs. Cap immediately. Store in a cool, dark place or in the refrigerator to retain the best flavor.

> **tip** ✣ Marjoram, opal basil, burnet, chive blossoms, tarragon, thyme, nasturtiums, rosemary, lavender, and rose petals are best with white wine vinegars. For red wine vinegar, choose strongly flavored herbs, such as basil, dill, garlic, sage, fennel, lovage, spearmint or peppermint, bay, thyme, chives, caraway, or savory.

Herb Jellies

Herb jellies provide yet another way to preserve herbs. Mint jelly is a traditional accompaniment to lamb, but the possible combinations are infinite. Thyme jellies are delicious with beef or fish; sage jelly goes well with poultry; basil jelly goes well with just about any meal.

If you are making apple jelly anyway, consider adding a few herb leaves to each hot, sterilized jar for an exciting new flavor. Otherwise, you will need to start with an herb infusion — herbs that have been steeped in a hot liquid for about 20 minutes. You may use homemade or commercial fruit juice or water as the base.

Please note: Please review the instructions for making jams and jellies in chapter 8 before proceeding with the recipe.

Basic Herb Jelly
Makes 6 half-pint jars

> 2 cups fruit juice or water
> 1 cup fresh herbs
> 2 tablespoons lemon juice
> 3½ cups sugar
> Few drops food coloring (optional)
> 1 pouch liquid pectin
> 6 fresh herb sprigs (optional)

① Begin preheating water in the boiling-water-bath canner and teakettle. Sterilize half-pint jars and prepare lids.

② In a saucepan, combine the fruit juice or water with the herbs. Heat to the boiling point, but do not boil. Remove from the heat, cover the pan, and let steep for 20 minutes. Strain the liquid through a coffee filter paper or a jelly bag, squeezing the herbs left in the paper or bag to extract all flavor. Discard the herbs.

③ In a large saucepan, combine the herb infusion, lemon juice, sugar, and food coloring. Bring to a full rolling boil over high heat, stirring constantly.

④ When the boil cannot be stirred down, pour in the pectin, stirring constantly. Boil for 1 minute. Remove from the heat. Stir and skim off any foam that collects on top.

⑤ Add 1 herb sprig to each sterilized jar. Immediately pour in the hot jelly, leaving ¼-inch headspace. Seal.

⑥ Process in a boiling-water bath for 5 minutes.

Preserving Each Herb

Anise

Harvest anise seed when it begins to dry on the plant. Dry seed stalks in a dehydrator at 110°F for 10 to 12 hours, or in a conventional oven at 110°F for 18 to 24 hours, or outdoors out of direct sunlight for several days. Remove seeds, discard stalks, and store.

USES. Use the licorice-flavored seeds in herb teas and baking.

Basil

Snip leaves from stems of sweet basil as soon as they have developed. Wash and pat dry. Dry leaves in a dehydrator or oven at 110°F for 8 to 12 hours. Dry stems outdoors for 1 to 2 days.

USES. To prepare Italian dishes and recipes with tomatoes, fish, cheese, and eggs. Delicious in herbal vinegars and jelly.

Chervil

Pick small bunches from immature plants. Dry in a dehydrator or oven at 110°F for 12 to 18 hours, or outdoors out of direct sunlight for several days. Crumble leaves, discard stems, and store.

USES. To flavor egg and cheese dishes.

Preserving
Herbs

131

Chives

Harvest chives before flowers form. Their flavor is best retained using one of the freezing methods detailed on pages 125 to 127. Or chop stems and dry in a dehydrator or oven at 110° F for 4 to 6 hours, or outdoors out of direct sunlight for 8 to 10 hours. Store.

USES. To flavor soups, salads, casseroles, sauces, herbal vinegars and jellies, and as a garnish.

Dill

Harvest dill for leaves when the plants are immature. Harvest heads as soon as flower buds form, but before all the buds are open. Dill heads can be bagged and frozen for use in pickles. Fresh dill weed can be frozen by any of the methods listed on pages 125 to 127. Dry finely chopped leaves in a dehydrator or conventional oven at 110°F for 6 to 8 hours; dry seeds for 4 to 6 hours at 120°F. Dry stems outdoors for 3 to 4 days. Dry seeds on trays outdoors in direct sun for 4 to 6 hours.

USES. To flavor egg, fish, and cheese dishes, as well as pickles and fresh salads. Makes excellent vinegar.

Fennel

Pick immature fennel leaves in the morning after the dew has dried. Fennel seed is harvested after it has dried somewhat in the pod, but before the seedpods burst. Freeze leaves by any of the methods listed on pages 125 to 127. Dry finely chopped leaves in a dehydrator or conventional oven at 110°F for 6 to 8 hours; dry seeds for 4 to 6 hours at 120°F. Dry stems outdoors for 3 to 4 days. Dry seeds on trays outdoors in direct sun for 4 to 6 hours.

USES. To flavor baked goods. Use seeds in herb teas.

Marjoram

Pick the leaves at maturity. Dry leaves in a dehydrator or conventional oven at 110°F for 6 to 8 hours. Dry leaves outdoors out of direct sunlight for 8 to 12 hours.

USES. To flavor meat and in bouquet garni.

Mint

Pick the leaves in early summer, when leaves are most fragrant. Dry leaves in a dehydrator or conventional oven at 110°F for 6 to 8 hours. Dry outdoors for 8 to 12 hours. Or freeze by any of the methods listed on page 125 to 127.

USES. Delightful in teas, jellies, vegetable dishes, and desserts.

Oregano

Pick the leaves just as the flowers open. Dry leaves in a dehydrator at 110°F for 4 to 8 hours or in a conventional oven at 110°F for 6 to 8 hours. Dry leaves outdoors out of direct sunlight for 8 to 12 hours.

USES. To flavor Italian dishes and meats, and in preparing seasoning mixes.

Parsley

Cut parsley tops with scissors as soon as new leaves have formed, and harvest throughout the season. You can freeze whole sprigs or finely chopped leaves by any of the methods explained on pages 125 to 127. Dry sprigs in a dehydrator at 110°F for 8 to 12 hours or chopped leaves for 6 to 8 hours. Or dry in a conventional oven at 110°F for 8 to 12 hours. Dry leaves outdoors out of direct sunlight for 8 to 10 hours.

USES. Add to any recipe. Use in bouquet garnis and as a garnish.

Rosemary

Harvest young leaves as soon as the aroma has developed. Dry whole or chopped leaves leaves in a dehydrator at 110°F for 6 to 8 hours. Or dry in a conventional oven at 110°F for 8 to 12 hours. Dry leaves outdoors out of direct sunlight for 8 to 10 hours.

USES. In cooking, especially with meats. In teas and hair rinses.

Sage

Pick the leaves at maturity. Dry leaves in a dehydrator at 110°F for 8 to 12 hours. Dry leaves in a conventional oven at 110°F for 10 to 12 hours. Or dry leaves outdoors out of direct sunlight for 10 to 14 hours.

USES. In cooking, especially with sausage, cheese, and poultry. Also in teas.

Tarragon

Pick the leaves when the plants are young. Dry the leaves in dehydrator at 110°F for 6 to 8 hours. Dry leaves in a conventional oven at 110°F for 8 to 12 hours. Or dry leaves outdoors out of direct sunlight for 8 to 12 hours.

USES. In cooking, especially with tomato dishes, and poultry. Also to flavor vinegar and herbal jellies.

Thyme

Pick the leaves when the plants first begin to flower. Dry the leaves in a dehydrator or conventional oven at 110°F for 6 to 8 hours. Or dry leaves outdoors out of direct sunlight for 8 to 12 hours.

USES. In cooking, especially with Italian dishes, meats, stews, and wild game. Also to flavor teas, vinegar, and herbal jellies.

CHAPTER 7

Pickles, Relishes, Sauerkraut, and Sauces

VARIETY IS THE SPICE OF LIFE, and pickles and relishes spice up many of my home-cooked meals.

You can find many books on pickles and relishes, but the following recipes are both speedy and practical, written with busy people in mind. Here's a great time-saving tip: Prepare my Busy Person's Relish-Sauce-Chutney recipe (page 148). Can half and save half. To the saved half, add peach preserves to make a great tasting sweet-and-sour sauce. Can half of that. To the half remaining, add nuts and raisins and end up with a marvelous chutney (so good I like to eat it right out of the jar!). Three different sauces out of one basic recipe — that's the kind of shortcut I hope you'll experiment with in your kitchen.

Pickles

TRADITIONALLY, cooks have used three basic methods to make pickles: fermenting in salt, used most commonly for dill pickles and sauerkraut; fresh-pack, quick-processed pickles, which can turn vegetables into spicy sweet or sour pickles; and relishes, made by chopping or grinding a mixture of vegetables, adding seasonings, vinegar, and sweeteners, and cooking to the desired consistency. Another option is freezer pickles. These are the easiest to make, but if your freezer space is at a premium, you will find the other recipes in this section are quick and easy to make as well.

BASIC INGREDIENTS FOR MAKING PICKLES

❋ **Vegetables and fruit.** These should be blemish-free, firm, and fresh. Small slender cucumbers and zucchini make the best whole pickles. Medium-size cucumbers or zucchini make good sliced pickles. Larger vegetables that have gone past their prime can be used to make relishes and sauces. Do not use waxed cucumbers; brine cannot penetrate the wax coating. Be sure to remove all blossom ends from the cucumbers; otherwise an enzyme in these blossoms may cause the pickles to soften during fermentation.

❋ **Salt.** Use pure coarse salt, pickling salt, or kosher salt for quick process pickles and relishes. When fermenting or using a recipe that states the salt is important to the preservation, use only the salt specified. Iodized salt will darken pickles and should not be used.

❋ **Vinegar.** Use high-quality vinegar of at least 5 percent acidity. (Don't use homemade vinegars.) Cider vinegar gives pickles a mellow, fruity taste and will produce a darker pickle. While distilled vinegar gives a sharper, more acid taste, it is best to use if you want light-colored pickles. Never reduce the amount of vinegar called for in a recipe. Weakening the vinegar could enable bacteria to grow in the brine. If a less sour taste is desired, add additional sweetener.

❋ **Sweeteners.** Use either white or brown sugar, or honey. Brown sugar will produce a darker pickle. Honey usually will cloud the brine.

✹ **Spices.** Use only fresh spices. Old spices may cause the pickles to taste musty. Whole spices are recommended over powdered. The whole spices should be loosely tied in a cheesecloth or small muslin bag and removed from the brine before packing the pickles in jars to prevent discoloration. However, many of the best cooks I know put the spices right into the brine and pack them with the pickles. The flavor of the spice is stronger, and the color is darker but not unpleasantly so.

✹ **Firming agents.** In the old days, many cooks used alum or grape leaves added to the brine or packed in the jar to produce a crisp pickle. These firming agents aren't necessary if fresh produce is used and recipes are followed carefully.

pickles and crock

EQUIPMENT

The equipment needed for making pickles is similar to that required for canning. Do not use copper, brass, galvanized, iron, or aluminum pots or utensils. These metals will react with the acids and salt used in pickles, causing color and taste changes.

Here is the list of equipment you will need: sharp paring knives, a scrub brush, large bowls, measuring cups and spoons, a colander, fine sieves, cheesecloth, a cutting board, crocks or large glass jars, a heavy plate, clean jars, a steam or boiling-water-bath canner, a preserving kettle or large roaster, a pan containing screw bands and lids in hot water, a widemouthed funnel, a ladle, large wooden and slotted spoons, a timer, hot pads, towels, a jar lifter, and a nonmetallic spatula for expelling bubbles from jars.

Before you start making pickles, be sure your work area and all equipment are spotlessly clean. Prewash your jars and check them for nicks and cracks.

PROCESSING

The USDA recommends that all pickles be processed in a boiling-water bath for long-term storage. If you feel that processing alters the texture of your pickles, then you may keep unprocessed pickles in the refrigerator for a few weeks. I definitely do not recommend storing unprocessed pickles on a shelf.

MAKING PICKLES: Fifteen Steps

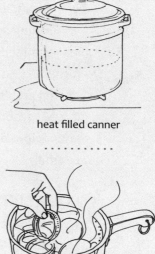

1 Preheat the canner, jars, and lids while preparing the recipe. To preheat a boiling-water-bath canner, fill it with 4 to 4½ inches of hot tap water. Set the jars on a rack inside the canner, bottom sides up. Turn the heat on high. If pickles are to be processed for 10 minutes or less, sterilize jars by boiling them in the canner for 10 minutes. Leave the jars in the hot water until needed. Prepare the lids according to the manufacturer's directions.

heat filled canner

preheat lids

2 Wash your vegetables thoroughly.

3 Prepare the vegetables according to the recipe.

4 Add seasonings, sweeteners, and vinegar to the vegetables, according to the recipe directions.

5 Cook, if necessary.

6 Pack the vegetables firmly in the hot jars, making sure that the pickling brine fills the jars to the level indicated in the recipe.

7 Release any air bubbles in the jars by inserting the spatula and running it between the contents and the side of the jars.

add brine

8 Add more brine, if needed, to maintain proper headspace.

9 Wipe the rim of the jars with a clean, damp cloth to remove any food particles, seeds, or spices.

10 Adjust the lids as the manufacturer recommends.

11 Place the filled jars on a rack in the preheated boiling-water-bath canner (140°F for raw-pack foods and 180°F for hot-pack foods). Make sure the water covers the jars by at least 2 inches. Cover the canner and bring the water to a boil.

12 Process for the length of time indicated in the individual recipe. Make sure the water is boiling throughout the processing time.

lower jar into canner

13 When processing time is up, turn off the heat, carefully remove the cover from the canner, and wait 5 minutes to help ensure proper sealing and avoid boil-overs from the jars. Using long-handled tongs or jar lifters, carefully remove jars from the canner. Place the jars several inches apart on a towel away from drafts.

   If the screw bands are loose, do not tighten them.

14 Cool the jars for 24 hours. Check the seals. Any jars not sealed should be refrigerated immediately and used within 2 weeks.

15 Remove screw bands, wipe sealed jars, label, date, and store in a cool, dry, dark place.

Pickles,
Relishes,
Sauerkraut,
and Sauces

139

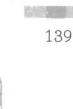

tip ❋ When opening each new jar, check for signs of spoilage: bulging lids, leakage, mold, bad odor, very soft or mushy pickles. If there is the slightest doubt in your mind, *do not taste*. Dispose of the pickles where no person or animal can access them. Wash and sterilize the jar before storing or reusing.

Recipes

BE SURE TO READ THROUGH EACH RECIPE before beginning, so you know whether you have time for the recipe. Some require leaving the vegetables in a salt brine for as little as 1 hour or as much as 10 days.

Note: Prewash your jars and make the pickling brine ahead of time. Heat the brine and can the cucumbers as they come along, 2 or 3 quarts at a time.

Quick Dill Pickles
Makes 3 quarts

> 3 cups white vinegar
> 3 cups water
> ⅓ cup pickling salt
> 4 pounds cucumbers, washed and cut into spears
> 6 heads dill, or 6 tablespoons dill seed
> 3 cloves garlic, peeled (optional)
> 9 peppercorns

① Preheat hot tap water in the canner; prepare jars and lids. In a saucepan, combine liquids and salt, and heat to boiling.

② Pack cucumbers into hot, clean quart jars. To each jar, add 2 heads dill, 1 clove garlic, if using, and 3 peppercorns.

③ Fill the jars with the hot pickling brine, leaving ½ inch of headroom. Adjust lids.

④ Process in a boiling-water bath for 20 minutes. Cool sealed jars. Check seals. Remove screw bands. Label. Store. For the best flavor, let the pickles stand and mellow for several weeks before eating.

Short-Brine Kosher Dill Pickles
Makes 7 quarts

6	tablespoons pickling salt
4	tablespoons sugar
6	cups cider vinegar
6	cups water
7	large grape leaves (optional)
2	tablespoons mixed pickling spices
16–17	pounds pickling cucumbers (3 to 5 inches long)
21	large heads dill or 7 tablespoons dill seed
14	cloves garlic
7	whole cayenne peppers (dried)

① Preheat hot tap water in the canner. Prepare quart jars and lids. In a saucepan, mix the salt, sugar, vinegar, water, and grape leaves, if using. Add the whole pickling spices tied in a spice bag. Heat to boiling. Meanwhile, scrub the cucumbers.

② Place 3 dill heads, 2 cloves garlic, and 1 cayenne pepper in each jar. Pack the cucumbers in the jars.

③ Fill the jars with hot brine to cover the cucumbers. Place 1 grape leaf (if using) in each jar. Leave ½-inch headspace.

④ Process for 15 minutes once water returns to a boil.

⑤ Cool sealed jars. Check seals. Remove screw bands. Label. Store.

Pickles,
Relishes,
Sauerkraut,
and Sauces

Sweet Chunk Pickles
Makes 4 pints

8 cucumbers, 5 inches long
½ cup pickling salt (or more)
4 cups white vinegar
4 cups water
2 large grape leaves (optional)
4 cups sugar
1 tablespoon mixed pickling spices

① Scrub the cucumbers. Place in a large nonreactive container and cover with cold salt brine made with ½ cup salt for each quart of cold water used. Let the cucumbers stand for 3 days.

② Drain. Cover with cold water. Let stand for 24 hours.

③ Repeat step 2 twice.

④ Combine 2 cups of the vinegar, 4 cups water, and grape leaves, if using, in a saucepan. Heat to boiling. Meanwhile, cut the cucumbers into ½-inch chunks. Pour the hot brine over the cucumbers. Let stand for 2 days.

⑤ Drain. Discard brine and grape leaves. Combine sugar, the remaining 2 cups vinegar, and spices in a saucepan. Heat to boiling. Pour over chunks. Let stand for 24 hours.

⑥ Pour off brine into a saucepan and heat to boiling. Pour hot brine over chunks. Let stand for 24 hours.

⑦ Repeat step 6. Let stand for 24 hours.

⑧ Fill the canner with hot tap water. Sterilize jars by boiling in the canner for 10 minutes. Prepare lids. Meanwhile, pour off brine into a saucepan and reheat to boiling.

(9) Pack the jars with pickles. Fill with hot brine. Leave ½-inch headspace.

(10) Process for 10 minutes once water has returned to a boil.

(11) Cool jars. Check seals. Remove screw bands. Label. Store.

Freezer Pickles
Makes 4 pints

30	cucumbers, 5 inches long (2 quarts sliced)
2	medium onions
2	tablespoons pickling salt
1½	cups sugar
1	cup cider vinegar
1	teaspoon celery seed

(1) Scrub and slice the cucumbers. Peel and thinly slice the onions. Combine in a large bowl and sprinkle with salt. Mix well.

(2) Cover bowl and let stand for 3 hours.

(3) Rinse the vegetables with cold tap water, and drain thoroughly. Return to the rinsed bowl. Meanwhile, mix sugar, vinegar, and celery seed in a separate bowl.

(4) Pour the brine over the vegetables. Mix, cover. Refrigerate overnight.

(5) Pack the pickles in straight-sided containers. Cover with brine. Leave 1-inch headspace. Seal. Freeze. Defrost in the refrigerator for 8 hours before serving.

Sunshine Pickles
Makes 7 pints

    3 cups sugar
    3 cups cider vinegar
    1 tablespoon pickling salt
    1 tablespoon celery seed
    3 large grape leaves (optional)
   10 firm cucumbers or zucchini, 6 to 8 inches long
       (5 quarts peeled and seeded)
    4 large onions
    1 tablespoon turmeric

① Combine the sugar, vinegar, salt, celery seed, and grape leaves, if using, in a preserving kettle. Heat on low while preparing cucumbers.

② Peel and seed cucumbers; cut into diagonal slices (2½- to 3-inch slices). Peel and slice the onions.

③ Place the vegetables in the hot brine. Bring to a boil; reduce heat and simmer until translucent. Meanwhile, fill the canner with hot tap water. Sterilize jars by boiling in the canner for 10 minutes. Prepare lids.

④ Remove the grape leaves from the brine; add the turmeric. Stir well. Pack the pickles in jars and fill with hot brine. Leave ½-inch headspace. (If pickling zucchinis, add ⅓ grape leaf to each jar.)

⑤ Process for 10 minutes once water has returned to a boil.

⑥ Cool jars. Check seal. Remove screw bands. Label. Store.

Sour Pickles

Makes 7 to 8 pints

Larger, slender cucumbers can be used for this recipe, but they should be cut in small chunks or spears.

> 2 quarts cider vinegar
> ½ cup dry mustard
> ½ cup sugar
> ½ cup pickling salt

60–80 scrubbed tiny cucumbers (1½ to 2½ inches long)

① Combine the vinegar, mustard, sugar, and salt. Pour into a clean gallon jar or container.

② Add the cucumbers. Let stand for 7 days in a cool place.

③ Fill the canner with hot tap water. Sterilize jars by boiling in the canner for 10 minutes. Prepare lids. Meanwhile, drain the pickles and save the brine. Pack the pickles in the jars. Fill the jars with the saved brine to cover the pickles. Leave ½-inch headspace.

④ Process for 10 minutes in the preheated boiling-water-bath canner. Start counting time as soon as water returns to boiling.

⑤ Cool sealed jars. Check seals. Remove screw bands. Label. Store.

tip ❖ If you do not have enough small pickles for a full batch, pick the cucumbers daily as they come along and add to the brine. After each gallon jar is filled, let it stand 7 days before processing in pints. Process pints for 10 minutes.

Dilly Beans
Makes 4 pints

- 2½ cups vinegar
- 2½ cups water
- ¼ cup pickling salt
- 2 pounds green beans, trimmed
- 1 teaspoon cayenne pepper
- 4 cloves garlic
- 4 heads dill

① Preheat hot tap water in the canner and teakettle. Prepare lids. Sterilize pint-size canning jars.

② In a saucepan, mix the vinegar, water, and salt. Heat to boiling.

③ Pack the beans in hot jars, leaving ½-inch headspace. To each pint, add ¼ teaspoon cayenne, 1 clove garlic, and 1 head dill. Pour hot liquid over beans, leaving ¼-inch headspace.

④ Process for 10 minutes once water has returned to a boil.

⑤ Cool jars. Check seals. Remove screw bands. Label. Store.

Pickled Beets

Makes 7 pints

pickled beets

10–12 pounds beets
    1 quart cider vinegar
    ⅔ cup sugar
    1 cup water
    2 tablespoons pickling salt

① Cut the tops and roots off flush with the beets. Scrub thoroughly.

② Place the beets on a rack in a large roaster. Cover and bake at 400°F until tender, about 1 hour for medium-sized beets. Meanwhile, preheat hot tap water and jars in the canner. Prepare lids.

③ In a saucepan, mix the vinegar, sugar, water, and salt. Heat to boiling.

④ When the beets are tender, fill the roaster with cold water. When cool enough to handle, slip the skins of the beets.

⑤ Pack the beets, whole or cut, in hot jars. Add brine to cover. Leave ½-inch headspace.

⑥ Process for 30 minutes once water has returned to a boil.

⑦ Cool jars. Check seals. Remove screw bands. Label. Store.

Pickles,
Relishes,
Sauerkraut,
and Sauces

147

Busy Person's Relish-Sauce-Chutney

Makes 14 pints and 7 half-pints

This recipe makes three great-tasting sauces: Indian Relish, a spicy sauce to eat with meats (makes a great Thousand Island salad dressing); Sweet-and-Sour Sauce, to use with meat, poultry, and seafood (especially good with Chinese or Polynesian dishes); and Chutney, fantastic with everything. It's very easy to make, but takes a little longer than other recipes. This is a good project for a free day.

Relish

24 large tomatoes (4 quarts purée)	⅔ cup pickling salt
24 large apples	2 teaspoons ground cloves
18 large onions (7 cups chopped)	2 teaspoons crushed red pepper flakes
2 quarts cider vinegar	2 teaspoons cinnamon
6 cups sugar	2 teaspoons dry mustard

Sweet-and-Sour Additions

7 cups peach preserves
2 teaspoons garlic powder
1 teaspoon Tabasco sauce

Chutney Additions

1 cup raisins
1 cup chopped walnuts

① Purée tomatoes in a hand-cranked strainer to make 4 quarts. Peel, core, and coarsely chop apples. Peel and chop onions to make 7 cups. Mix in a large roaster or preserving kettle with vinegar, sugar, salt, cloves, red pepper, cinnamon, and dry mustard.

② Bring to a boil and simmer until thick, about 2 hours. Meanwhile, fill the canner with hot tap water sterlize jars by boiling the canner for 10 minutes. Prepare lids.

③ Ladle hot sauce into 7 hot pint-size jars. Leave ½-inch headspace.

④ Process for 10 minutes once water has returned to a boil. While the jars are processing, add the peach preserves, garlic powder, and Tabasco to the remaining sauce and reheat to boiling.

⑤ Fill 7 pint-size jars, leaving ½-inch headspace. Remove the relish jars and reheat the canner.

⑥ Process the jars for 10 minutes once water returns to a boil. While the jars are processing, add the raisins and nuts to the remaining sauce, and reheat to boiling. Remove the sweet-and-sour jars and reheat the canner.

⑦ Pack the hot chutney into 7 half-pint jars. Leave ½-inch headspace.

⑧ Process for 10 minutes once water returns to a boil.

⑨ Cool jars. Check seals. Remove screw bands. Label. Store.

Freezer Coleslaw
Makes about 4 pints

    1 medium cabbage
    1 carrot
    1 green pepper
    2 tablespoons pickling salt
    1 cup cider vinegar
1¼ cups sugar
  ¼ cup water
    1 teaspoon celery seed

① Shred the cabbage, carrot, and green pepper. Sprinkle with salt; mix well. Cover. Let stand for 1 hour.

② Meanwhile, mix the vinegar, sugar, water, and celery seed in a saucepan. Bring to a boil. Boil 1 minute.

③ Rinse the vegetables with cold tap water and drain. Squeeze out as much water as possible.

④ Pour the brine over the cabbage mixture. Stir well. Cool.

⑤ Pack in straight-sided containers. Leave 1-inch headspace. Seal. Freeze. Defrost and store in the refrigerator before serving.

German Pickle Relish
Makes about 7 pints

2 quarts finely chopped or ground cabbage	1 tablespoon pickling salt
	¼ teaspoon pepper
1 quart ground green tomatoes	12 whole cloves
	½ cup mustard seed
2 sweet red peppers, finely chopped	4½ cups sugar
	1 quart cider vinegar
1 quart sliced onions	1 teaspoon turmeric
1 tablespoon celery seed	

① Mix together the cabbage, green tomatoes, peppers, and onions.

② Combine the vegetables with the remaining ingredients, except turmeric, in a large saucepan. Heat to boiling. Simmer until cabbage is very tender (about 1 hour). Meanwhile, fill the canner with hot tap water. Prepare lids. Sterilize jars by boiling in canner for 10 minutes.

③ Remove relish from the heat when done. Stir in turmeric.

④ Pack the relish in hot jars. Leave 1-inch headspace.

⑤ Put filled jars in preheated canner. Process for 10 minutes once water has returned to a boil.

⑥ Cool jars. Check seals. Remove screw bands. Label. Store.

Zucchini Relish
Makes about 7 pints

  5 tablespoons pickling salt
 10 cups finely chopped zucchini
  4 cups finely chopped onions
  1 green pepper, finely chopped
  1 red pepper, finely chopped
2½ cups white vinegar
  1 large cayenne pepper with seeds
  1 tablespoon nutmeg
  1 tablespoon dry mustard
  1 tablespoon turmeric
  1 tablespoon cornstarch
  ½ teaspoon pepper
  2 teaspoons celery salt
4½ cups sugar

① Sprinkle salt over the vegetables in a large bowl. Mix well. Let stand overnight.

② Drain the vegetables. Rinse thoroughly with cold tap water. Drain again.

③ Place the vegetables in a large kettle with the remaining ingredients. (Purée the cayenne pepper in blender with a little of the vinegar for better flavor.) Bring to a boil. Simmer for 30 to 45 minutes until thick. Meanwhile fill the canner with hot tap water. Prepare lids. Sterilize jars by boiling in canner for 10 minutes.

④ Pack jars. Leave ½-inch headspace.

⑤ Process for 10 minutes once water has returned to a boil.

⑥ Cool jars. Check seals. Remove screw bands. Label. Store.

Pickles,
Relishes,
Sauerkraut,
and Sauces

151

Sauerkraut

Makes 7 pints

   5 **pounds cabbage**
   3 **tablespoons pickling salt**
 12 **juniper berries**
 ½ **cup dry white wine**

① Shred the cabbage. Layer the cabbage, salt, and juniper berries (3 per layer) in a large crock or bowl that holds at least 1 gallon. Tap every other layer with a potato masher to get rid of trapped air bubbles. Cover with a clean cloth and weigh down with a heavy plate. Place a jar or can on the plate, if necessary. Place this container in another pan to collect fermenting juices that overflow. Place in an area that remains between 65°F and 75°F.

② By the next day, brine will form and cover the cabbage. By the second day, scum will start to form. On the second day, pour the wine over everything.

    Rinse the plate and cloth and replace each day.

③ Skim any scum that has formed after 2 weeks.

④ Skim again after 4 weeks.

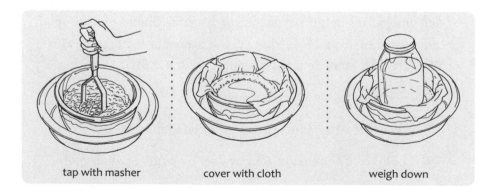

tap with masher   cover with cloth   weigh down

(5) To can (hot-pack only), fill the canner with hot tap water and preheat water in jars in canner. Prepare lids.

While the canner and jars are preheating, heat the sauerkraut to simmer. Do not boil. Pack in hot jars. Leave ½-inch headspace. If you run short of juice, mix a brine of 1½ tablespoons pickling salt to 1 quart boiling water. (Divide this mixture between the jars; do not use the new brine to fill just 1 jar.)

(6) Put filled jars in the preheated canner. Process 10 minutes for pints, 15 minutes for quarts, once water has returned to a boil.

(7) Cool jars. Check seals. Remove screw bands. Label. Store.

Sauerkraut can be stored in a crock, and not canned, if the area in which it is stored remains at a constant 38°F. When removing a portion of sauerkraut from the crock, make sure the remaining sauerkraut is covered with brine. Mix more brine, 1½ tablespoons of pickling salt to 1 quart water, if necessary. Always use a glass or china (not metal) cup to remove a portion of sauerkraut.

How can you tell if sauerkraut is spoiled? Spoiled sauerkraut has an off odor and changes in color. Soft kraut is caused by insufficient salt, uneven distribution of salt, temperature too high during fermentation, or unexpelled air bubbles when packing. Pink kraut indicates a yeast growth on the surface, too much or improperly distributed salt, or improper weighting during fermentation. Rotted kraut is caused by an insufficient covering of brine to exclude air. Dark kraut is caused by cabbage that was washed or trimmed improperly; insufficient covering of brine to exclude air; poor distribution of salt; high fermentation, processing, or storage temperatures; or too much time in storage.

Jan's Spicy Spaghetti Sauce
Makes 6 to 7 quarts

30	pounds tomatoes (10 quarts purée)
4	large onions
⅓	cup dried sweet basil
2	tablespoons dried oregano
1	teaspoon dried thyme
1	teaspoon pepper
¾	cup honey or sugar (optional)
1	teaspoon dried marjoram
5	bay leaves
1	tablespoon crushed red pepper
1	tablespoon garlic powder
2	tablespoons salt
1½	tablespoons dried parsley
3–3½	teaspoons citric acid

① Preheat oven to 200°F. Purée tomatoes in a hand-cranked strainer. Chop onion finely. Put the vegetables with remaining ingredients except citric acid in a large roaster. Stir well. Bring to a boil on top of the stove.

② Cook, uncovered, in the oven for 10 hours. Do not stir.

③ One hour before cooking time is up, fill the canner with hot tap water and preheat water and jars in the canner. Prepare lids.

④ When cooking time is up, ladle the hot sauce into hot jars. Leave ½-inch headspace. Add ½ teaspoon citric acid to each jar to ensure the safety of the sauce.

⑤ Process 35 minutes for pints and quarts once water has returned to a boil.

⑥ Cool jars. Check seals. Remove screw bands. Label. Store.

tip ✣ Citric acid is added to seasoned tomato sauces to guarantee that the sauce is acidic enough to be canned safely in a boiling-water bath. Citric acid is available from your drugstore and will not affect the flavor of the sauce. Instead of citric acid, you can use 2 tablespoons of fresh lemon juice per quart of sauce.

Spicy Salsa
Makes about 7 pints

- 5 pounds tomatoes
- 2 pounds hot chili peppers
- 1 pound onions
- 1 cup cider vinegar
- 3 teaspoons salt
- ½ teaspoon pepper

① Fill the canner with hot tap water and preheat water and jars in canner. Prepare lids.

② Purée tomatoes in a hand-cranked strainer. Finely chop chili peppers and onions. Put all the ingredients in a large saucepan. Bring to a boil, then simmer for 10 minutes.

③ Ladle the hot sauce into hot jars. Leave ½-inch headspace.

④ Put the filled jars in the preheated canner. Process pints for 15 minutes once water has returned to a boil.

⑤ Cool jars. Check seals. Remove screw bands. Label. Store.

Just Like Store-Bought Ketchup
Makes 12 pints

24 pounds tomatoes (8 quarts purée)
12 ounces thick tomato paste
 3 green peppers, seeded and chopped
 5 large onions, peeled and chopped
 3 cups cider vinegar
 1 cup light corn syrup
 1 cup sugar
 1 teaspoon pepper
 2 tablespoons salt
 2 teaspoons ground allspice

① Preheat oven to 200°F. Purée the tomatoes with a hand-cranked strainer. Liquefy the tomato paste, peppers, and onions in a blender with some of the vinegar. Mix the purée with remaining ingredients in a large roaster. Stir well. Bring to a boil on top of the stove.

② Cook, uncovered, in the oven for 10 hours. Do not stir.

③ One hour before cooking time is up, fill the canner with hot tap water and preheat water and jars in canner. Prepare lids.

④ When cooking time is up, ladle the hot ketchup into the hot pint jars. Leave ½-inch headspace.

⑤ Process pints for 15 minutes once water has returned to a boil.

⑥ Cool jars. Check seals. Remove screw bands. Label. Store.

> **tip** ❈ Spaghetti sauce and ketchup can be reduced on top of the stove by cooking for 3 hours, but you must stir often to avoid boiling over or sticking. Sauces cooked in the oven take longer to reduce; they do not need to be stirred. They will not boil over, nor will they stick to the pot. To hurry the process toward the end, you can quickly reduce the sauce by cooking it for a very short period of time on top of the stove.

Kate's Fresh Salsa
Makes 2 cups

    2 large tomatoes, chopped and seeded
    1 medium Vidalia or sweet onion, chopped
    2 tablespoons lime juice (2 limes)
    ⅓ cup chopped fresh cilantro
    2 tablespoons chopped green chilies
    2 drops Tabasco sauce
      Salt
      Freshly ground pepper

① Mix all ingredients in a medium bowl. Let stand for 30 minutes to blend the flavors.

② If you make the salsa ahead of time, leave out the chilies until just before serving.

Pickles,
Relishes,
Sauerkraut,
and Sauces

157

Ten Commonly Asked Questions About Pickling

Q **Must I process pickles and relishes?**

A Yes. The USDA now recommends processing all pickles and relishes to ensure destruction of harmful bacteria.

Q **Must I sterilize jars when I process pickles and relishes?**

A To process pickles and relishes, it is not necessary to sterilize jars, if you process for 10 minutes or more in a boiling-water bath.

Q **What causes soft or slippery pickles?**

A Not using freshly picked cucumbers, too little salt in the brine, acidity of vinegar is less than 5 percent, reducing the acid strength of the vinegar by adding more water than the recipe called for, not removing scum regularly, vegetables not covered with brine, hard water, not removing blossom ends from cucumbers, processing too long, or storing pickles where it is too warm.

Q **What causes hollow pickles?**

A Growing conditions (long dry spells followed by heavy rains), cucumbers stored too long before pickling, brine not strong enough, or high fermentation temperatures.

Q **What causes shriveled pickles?**

A Cucumbers stored too long before pickling, pickling solution too sweet or vinegar too strong, not enough salt in the brine, cooking too long, or processing too long.

Q **Why do my pickles become dull or faded?**

A Poor quality cucumbers, sunburned or overmature cucumbers, or poor growing conditions.

Q **What causes dark pickles?**
A Using too much spice, not removing whole spices from brine before packing pickles, minerals in the water (hard water), over-cooking, cooking in an iron kettle, using iodized salt, or low nitrogen content of cucumbers.

Q **What causes the white sediment that collects in the bottom of my jars of pickles?**
A Bacteria caused by fermentation, fluctuations in storage temperatures, or not using pure canning salt. It is usually not harmful unless the pickles are spoiled. If the pickles are spoiled, the jars frequently will spurt liquid when opened.

Q **What causes pickles to spoil?**
A Not following directions carefully for packing and processing, using ingredients that are too old, or weakening the vinegar solution by adding more water than the recipe called for.

Q **When I add whole garlic to my dills the garlic turns blue. Why?**
A This is not unusual. Hard water, which is high in minerals, is usually the cause. Garlic naturally contains sulfur compounds. When these compounds come in contact with copper, even a small amount of copper, they react to form copper sulfate, which is blue or blue-green. The color will not affect the taste.

Pickles,
Relishes,
Sauerkraut,
and Sauces

CHAPTER 8

Jams, Jellies, Preserves, and Marmalades

MANY JAM-MAKING METHODS don't involve working long hours in a hot kitchen. Freezer jams and jellies take much of the work out of preserving. These involve very little cooking — just enough to allow the pectin mixture and sugar to dissolve in the fruit juice. Another trick is to save your jam- and jelly-making for later in the season when the weather is cooler. You can make preserves from frozen or canned fruit, instead of fresh.

Never double recipes for preserves — the product will not gel properly. It is important to follow the recipe carefully and precisely. If you are using a commercial pectin, then exact measuring and timing are critical; if you are making a preserve without added pectin, then using a thermometer to gauge when the product has reached the gel point is safest.

IF YOU ARE NEW TO MAKING PRESERVES, start by making jams with added pectin. They are easy and fairly fail-proof. Graduate to making jams and other preserves without added pectin.

If all you want is a satisfactory spread to go with peanut butter, there is no need to go beyond jams. I include jelly-making here because sometimes you just want to have jelly. But be forewarned — the process is more time-consuming. I recommend using commercial pectin when making jelly, as there are many pitfalls along the way without it.

Types of Preserves

BASICALLY, YOU CAN CHOOSE FROM SIX TYPES of jellied fruit products — all called preserves. *Jellies* are usually made by cooking clear fruit juice with sugar. They should hold their shape on a spoon but be soft enough to spread on toast. *Jams* are thick, sweet spreads made from cooked and crushed fruit and sugar. They are less firm than jelly. *Preserves* are made with small pieces of fruit suspended in a clear, slightly gelled syrup. *Conserves* are jams that are made from fruit combinations. Sometimes they contain raisins, nuts, or coconut. *Marmalades* are soft fruit jellies that contain small pieces of fruit or peel evenly suspended in a clear jelly. *Butters* are fruit pulp cooked down to a spreading consistency.

INGREDIENTS FOR MAKING PRESERVES

❋ **Fruit.** Fruit is the basis of most preserves. It doesn't have to be picture-perfect since it will be cut up, mashed, or made into juice. But the fruit should be of high quality and free from mold or any spoilage. You can make preserves from fresh, frozen, or canned fruit. If you are using frozen or canned fruit, be sure to take into account any sugar already added to the fruit. For the best results, it is safer to use unsweetened fruit.

Most fruits (with the notable exception of berries) can be held at room temperature for several days if you can't preserve right away.

❊ **Pectin.** Pectin is a substance that occurs naturally in fruit; it is what causes fruit juice to gel. Some fruits — most apples, grapes, blueberries, blackberries, cherries, cranberries, — have enough natural pectin to make high-quality preserves. Others require the addition of pectin to form a good gel. Commercial pectins are made from apples or citrus fruit and are available in both powdered and liquid forms. Be sure to follow the manufacturer's directions or tested recipes when using commercial pectin. The powdered and liquid forms are not interchangeable.

It may seem more natural to avoid using these commercial pectins — to make jams and jellies the old-fashioned way by cooking down fruit and sugar until you have a thick preserve — but I recommend commercial pectins for busy people for several reasons. First, fully ripe fruit can be used with these products, so when you harvest or when you get around to making your preserves is less critical. Second, cooking time is considerably shorter. Third, no guesswork is involved in terms of when the product is done. And finally, the yield is greater — more jars for your effort. If you have found that commercial pectins make a preserve that is too sweet for your taste, try one of the reduced-sugar pectins on the market.

❊ **Sugar.** Sugar is an important ingredient in preserves. It must be present in the right amount (along with some acid) to activate the pectin. It also acts as a preservative. If you reduce the amount of sugar in a recipe, you will probably not get a good gel. White sugar is the best sweetener for preserves, as it contributes sweetness without flavor. You can try using part honey or part corn syrup instead, but I don't recommend brown sugar or maple syrup as they contribute too much flavor.

❊ **Acid.** Acid is needed for both gelling and flavor. The acidity of fruit varies and is higher in underripe fruit. Most recipes call for the addition of lemon juice. Although the quantity is small, don't omit it.

EQUIPMENT

✳ The equipment needed for making preserves is similar to that required for canning. Do not use aluminum, brass, galvanized, or iron pots or utensils. These metals will react with the fruit, causing color and taste changes.

✳ In addition to the boiling-water bath, you will need a large saucepan that will hold 8 to 10 quarts, with a heavy bottom to prevent scorching and tall sides to prevent the mixture from boiling over. A jelly bag or suitable cloth is needed for extracting juice for jellies. A candy, jelly, or deep-fat thermometer is needed if you are making preserves without added pectin; if you are using commercial pectin, you will need a timer or a clock with a second hand.

PROCESSING

✳ Unless you plan to store your preserves in the refrigerator or freezer, you will need sterilized jars. Once filled, the jars should be processed in a boiling-water bath for 10 minutes.

JAM- AND PRESERVE-MAKING
(WITHOUT ADDED PECTIN): Fourteen Steps

1 Preheat the canner, and prepare the jars and lids.

Fill the boiling-water-bath canner with 4 to 4½ inches of hot tap water. Set the jars on a rack inside the canner, bottom sides up. Turn the heat on high and bring to a boil. Boil jars for 10 minutes. Then turn off the heat but leave the jars in the water until needed.

Wash and rinse all canning lids and screw bands. Treat the lids as directed by the manufacturer. Remember that lids can be used only once.

2 Wash the fruit thoroughly.

3 Prepare the fruit according to the recipe directions — chop, crush, and so on.

4 Combine the fruit in a tall, heavy saucepan with the sweetener and lemon juice according to the recipe directions.

5 Stir fruit over low heat until sugar dissolves. Then boil rapidly. As the mixture begins to thicken, stir frequently to prevent scorching.

6 Test for doneness. Use a candy, jelly, or deep-fat thermometer and boil until the temperature reaches 220°F, or 8 degrees above the boiling point of water.

7 Remove from heat and skim off any foam that formed during boiling.

8 Pour into the sterilized jars, leaving ¼-inch headspace.

9 Wipe the rims of the jars with a clean, damp cloth.

10 Adjust the lids as the manufacturer recommends.

11 Place the filled jars on a rack in the preheated canner. Make sure the water covers the jars by at least 2 inches. Cover the canner and bring the water to a boil. Process for 10 minutes once the water has returned to a boil.

12 When the processing time is up, carefully remove the jars from the canner, using a jar lifter.

13 Cool the jars for 24 hours. Check the seals. Any jars not sealed should be refrigerated immediately and used within 2 weeks.

14 Remove screw bands, wipe sealed jars, label, date, and store in a cool, dry, dark place.

tips ❖ If you don't have a jelly thermometer, you can test for gelling the old-fashioned way:

❖ *Sheet test.* Dip a cool metal spoon into the boiling fruit mixture and lift the spoon out of the steam so the syrup runs off the side. When the mixture first starts to boil, the drops will be light and syrupy. As the syrup continues to boil, the drops will become heavier and will drop off the spoon two at a time. When the jellying point has been reached, the two drops form together and "sheet" off the spoon.

❖ *Freezer test.* Pour a small amount of the boiling mixture on a plate and put it in the freezer for a few minutes. If the mixture gels, it is done. During this test, the rest of the recipe should be removed from the heat.

JAM- AND PRESERVE-MAKING (WITH ADDED PECTIN): Thirteen Steps

Note that these are general directions only. Follow the exact recipes that come in the package with the commercial pectin.

❶ Fill the boiling-water-bath canner with 4 to 4½ inches of hot tap water. Set the jars on a rack inside the canner, bottom sides up. Turn the heat on high and bring to a boil. Boil jars for 10 minutes. Then turn off the heat but leave the jars in the water until needed.

Wash and rinse all canning lids and screw bands. Treat the lids as directed by the manufacturer. Remember that lids can be used only once.

❷ Wash the fruit thoroughly.

❸ Prepare the fruit according to the recipe directions — chop, crush, and so on.

❹ Measure the sugar and set aside.

Jams, Jellies,
Preserves,
and
Marmalades

165

5 Combine the fruit and lemon juice in a tall, heavy saucepan. Add the pectin. Bring mixture to a full rolling boil that cannot be stirred down. Quickly add the sugar and return to a full rolling boil. Boil for 1 minute, stirring constantly.

6 Remove from heat and skim off any foam that formed during boiling.

7 Pour into the jars, leaving ¼-inch headspace.

8 Wipe the rims of the jars with a clean, damp cloth.

9 Adjust the lids as the manufacturer recommends.

10 Place the filled jars on a rack in the preheated canner. Make sure the water covers the jars by at least 2 inches. Cover the canner and bring the water to a boil. Process for 10 minutes once the water has returned to a boil.

11 When the processing time is up, carefully remove the jars from the canner, using a jar lifter.

12 Cool the jars for 24 hours. Check the seals. Any jars not sealed should be refrigerated immediately and used within 2 weeks.

13 Remove screw bands, wipe sealed jars, label, date, and store in a cool, dry, dark place.

JELLY-MAKING (WITHOUT ADDED PECTIN): Fifteen Steps

1 To ensure sufficient pectin for jelling, use 1 part slightly under-ripe fruit and 3 parts just-ripe fruit. Wash fruit. Do not remove skins or cores. Place fruit in a heavy-bottomed saucepan. To hard fruits, such as apples, add 1 cup of water per pound of fruit. For berries and grapes, use only enough water to prevent scorching. Crush soft fruits to start the flow of juice.

2 Bring to a boil over high heat. Stir frequently to prevent scorching. Reduce heat and simmer. Cook berries and grapes 10 minutes or less, until soft. Cook apples and other hard fruits for 20 to 25 minutes, until soft. Do not overcook.

3 Pour into a damp jelly bag or colander lined with a double thickness of damp cheesecloth. Allow the juice to filter out into a bowl.

4 Allow the juice to sit overnight so that any sediment can settle to the bottom. Do not squeeze fruit pulp as the resulting juice will not be clear.

5 When you are ready to make the jelly, preheat the canner, and prepare the jars and lids.

Fill the boiling-water-bath canner with 4 to 4½ inches of hot tap water. Set the jars on a rack inside the canner, bottom sides up. Turn the heat on high and bring to a boil. Boil jars for 10 minutes. Then turn off the heat but leave the jars in the water until needed.

Wash and rinse all canning lids and screw bands. Treat the lids as directed by the manufacturer. Remember that lids can be used only once.

6 Combine up to 4 cups of the clear fruit juice with sugar in a tall, heavy-bottomed saucepan, allowing ¾ cup sugar for each 1 cup of juice. Add 1 tablespoon lemon juice for each cup of fruit juice.

7 Stir to dissolve the sugar. Bring rapidly to a boil. Continue boiling until jelly reaches 220°F on a jelly thermometer or sheets off the spoon (see page 165).

8 Remove from heat and skim off any foam that formed during boiling.

9 Pour into the jars, leaving ¼-inch headspace.

10 Wipe the rims of the jars with a clean, damp cloth.

11 Adjust the lids as the manufacturer recommends.

12 Place the filled jars on a rack in the preheated canner. Make sure the water covers the jars by at least 2 inches. Cover the canner and bring the water to a boil. Process for 10 minutes once the water has returned to a boil.

13 When the processing time is up, carefully remove the jars from the canner, using a jar lifter.

14 Cool the jars for 24 hours. Check the seals. Any jars not sealed should be refrigerated immediately and used within 2 weeks.

15 Remove screw bands, wipe sealed jars, label, date, and store in a cool, dry, dark place.

JELLY-MAKING (WITH ADDED PECTIN): Fifteen Steps

Note that these fifteen steps are general directions only. Follow the exact recipes that come in the package with the commercial pectin. If you have already canned or frozen unsweetened fruit juice, you may use the juice and skip steps 1 to 4.

1 Wash fruit. Do not remove skins or cores. Place fruit in a heavy-bottomed saucepan. To hard fruits, such as apples, add 1 cup of water per pound of fruit. For berries and grapes, use only enough water to prevent scorching. Crush soft fruits to start the flow of juice.

2 Bring to a boil over high heat. Stir frequently to prevent scorching. Reduce heat and simmer. Cook berries and grapes 10 minutes or less, until soft. Cook apples and other hard fruits for 20 to 25 minutes, until soft. Do not overcook.

3 Pour into a damp jelly bag or colander lined with a double thickness of damp cheesecloth. Allow the juice to filter out into a bowl.

4 Allow the juice to sit overnight so that any sediment can settle to the bottom. Do not squeeze fruit pulp, as the resulting juice will not be clear.

5 When you are ready to make the jelly, preheat the canner, and prepare the jars and lids.

Fill the boiling-water-bath canner with 4 to 4½ inches of hot tap water. Set the jars on a rack inside the canner, bottom sides up. Turn the heat on high and bring to a boil. Boil jars for 10 minutes. Then turn off the heat but leave the jars in the water until needed.

Wash and rinse all canning lids and screw bands. Treat the lids as directed by the manufacturer. Remember that lids can be used only once.

6 Measure the sugar and set aside.

7 Measure the clear juice and mix with the pectin in a tall, heavy saucepan. Bring mixture to a boil. Quickly add the sugar and return to a full rolling boil. Boil for 1 minute, stirring constantly.

8 Remove from heat and skim off any foam that formed during boiling.

9 Pour into the jars, leaving ¼-inch headspace.

10 Wipe the rims of the jars with a clean, damp cloth.

11 Adjust the lids as the manufacturer recommends.

12 Place the filled jars on a rack in the preheated canner. Make sure the water covers the jars by at least 2 inches. Cover the canner and bring the water to a boil. Process for 10 minutes once the water has returned to a boil.

13 When the processing time is up, carefully remove the jars from the canner, using a jar lifter.

14 Cool the jars for 24 hours. Check the seals. Any jars not sealed should be refrigerated immediately and used within 2 weeks.

15 Remove screw bands, wipe sealed jars, label, date, and store in a cool, dry, dark place.

Jams, Jellies, Preserves, and Marmalades

Recipes

HERE ARE SOME BASIC RECIPES to get you started with preserves. None of these recipes do use commercial pectin. If you are in a rush, make your preserves with commercial pectin, following the recipes that are included in the package, and cut the cooking time to about 10 minutes, compared to 30 to 50 minutes for the majority of the jam recipes.

Fruits high in natural pectin

sour apples, sour blackberries, crabapples, cranberries, currants, gooseberries, grapes (Eastern Concord), lemons, loganberries, plums (not Italian), and quinces

Fruits low in natural pectin

apricots, figs, grapes (Western Concord), guavas, peaches, pears, plums (Italian), raspberries, and strawberries
When making preserves with these fruits, plan to use commercial pectin for best results.

tips ✳ Sometimes, despite your best efforts, a batch of jam, jelly, or preserves fails to gel. Don't call it a failure; call it a syrup and serve it on top of ice cream or pound cake.

✳ You may remember seeing jelly jars sealed with paraffin. The USDA no longer recommends this. All jams and jellies must be processed in a boiling-water bath to prevent mold.

Basic Grape Jelly
Makes 3 to 4 half-pint jars

- 3½ pounds grapes
- ½ cup water
- 3 cups sugar

① Wash the grapes; remove stems. Crush grapes and combine with water in a heavy-bottomed saucepan. Bring to a boil, then reduce the heat and simmer for 10 minutes.

② Pour into a damp jelly bag or colander lined with a double thickness of damp cheesecloth. Allow the juice to filter out into a bowl.

③ Allow the juice to sit overnight so that any sediment can settle to the bottom. Do not squeeze fruit pulp as the resulting juice will not be clear.

④ When you are ready to make the jelly, preheat the canner, sterilize the jars, and prepare the lids.

⑤ Combine 4 cups of sediment-free grape juice with the sugar in a tall, heavy-bottomed saucepan. Stir to dissolve the sugar.

⑥ Bring rapidly to a boil. Continue boiling until jelly reaches 220°F on a thermometer or sheets off the spoon (see page 165).

⑦ Remove from heat and skim off any foam.

⑧ Pour into the jars, leaving ¼-inch headspace. Wipe the rims of the jars with a clean, damp cloth. Adjust the lids as the manufacturer recommends.

⑨ Place the filled jars on a rack in the preheated canner and process for 10 minutes.

⑩ Cool sealed jars. Check seals. Remove screw bands. Label. Store.

Jams, Jellies,
Preserves,
and
Marmalades

Basic Peach Jam
Makes 7 to 8 half-pint jars

> 2 quarts peaches
> ½ cup water
> 6 cups sugar

1. Preheat the canner, sterilize the jars, and prepare the lids.

2. Prepare peaches. To peel peaches, dip in boiling water for 30 seconds. Then cool in ice water. Slip off skins. Remove pits. Crush by hand or pulse in a food processor.

3. Combine the peaches and water in a tall, heavy saucepan; boil for 10 minutes.

4. Add the sugar and bring slowly to a boil, stirring occasionally, until sugar dissolves. Then boil rapidly until thick, about 15 minutes. As the mixture begins to thicken, stir frequently to prevent scorching.

5. Test for doneness — 220°F on a thermometer or when the jam sheets off the spoon (see page 165).

6. Pour into the jars, leaving ¼-inch headspace. Wipe the rims of the jars with a clean, damp cloth. Adjust the lids as the manufacturer recommends.

7. Place the filled jars on a rack in the preheated canner. Process for 10 minutes once the water has returned to a boil.

8. When the processing time is up, carefully remove the jars from the canner using a jar lifter.

9. Cool sealed jars. Check seals. Remove screw bands. Label. Store.

Basic Berry Jam
Makes 7 to 8 half-pint jars

This recipe can be used with blackberries, blueberries, boysenberries, dewberries, gooseberries, loganberries, raspberries, and youngberries.

9 cups berries
6 cups sugar

① Preheat the canner, sterilize the jars, and prepare the lids.

② Wash berries carefully.

③ Combine the berries and sugar in a tall, heavy saucepan. Crush to break skins and release juices.

④ Bring slowly to a boil, stirring occasionally, until sugar dissolves. Then boil rapidly until thick, about 40 minutes. As the mixture begins to thicken, stir frequently to prevent scorching.

⑤ Test for doneness — 220°F on a thermometer or when the jam sheets off the spoon (see page 165).

⑥ Remove from heat and skim off any foam that formed during boiling.

⑦ Pour into the jars, leaving ¼-inch headspace. Wipe the rims of the jars with a clean, damp cloth. Adjust the lids as the manufacturer recommends.

⑧ Place the filled jars on a rack in the preheated canner. Process for 10 minutes once the water has returned to a boil.

⑨ When the processing time is up, carefully remove the jars from the canner, using a jar lifter.

⑩ Cool sealed jars. Check seals. Remove screw bands. Label. Store.

Jams, Jellies,
Preserves,
and
Marmalades

Basic Strawberry Jam
Makes 7 to 8 half-pint jars

2 quarts strawberries

6 cups sugar

(1) Preheat the canner, sterilize the jars, and prepare the lids.

(2) Wash and hull the berries carefully.

(3) Combine the berries and sugar in a tall, heavy saucepan. Crush to release juices.

(4) Bring slowly to a boil, stirring occasionally, until sugar dissolves. Then boil rapidly until thick, about 40 minutes. As the mixture begins to thicken, stir frequently to prevent scorching.

(5) Test for doneness — 220°F on a thermometer or when the jam sheets off the spoon (see page 165).

(6) Remove from heat and skim off any foam that formed during boiling.

(7) Pour into the jars, leaving ¼-inch headspace. Wipe the rims of the jars with a clean, damp cloth. Adjust the lids as the manufacturer recommends.

(8) Place the filled jars on a rack in a preheated canner. Process for 10 minutes once the water has returned to a boil.

(9) When the processing time is up, carefully remove the jars from the canner using a jar lifter.

(10) Cool sealed jars. Check seals. Remove screw bands. Label. Store.

Basic Strawberry Preserves
Makes about 4 half-pint jars

> 1½ quarts firm, ripe strawberries
> 5 cups sugar
> ⅓ cup lemon juice

① Wash the strawberries. Hull and remove stems. Combine strawberries and sugar in a tall, heavy-bottomed saucepan; let stand for 3 to 4 hours.

② Bring the strawberries and sugar slowly to a boil, stirring occasionally, until sugar dissolves. Add lemon juice. Boil rapidly until the berries are soft and the syrup is clear, about 10 to 12 minutes.

③ Pour into a shallow pan. Let stand, uncovered, for 12 to 24 hours in a cool place. Shake pan occasionally to distribute the berries through the syrup.

④ Preheat the canner, sterilize the jars, and prepare the lids.

⑤ Heat preserves until boiling. Pour hot preserves into the jars, leaving ¼-inch headspace. Wipe the rims of the jars with a clean, damp cloth. Adjust the lids as the manufacturer recommends.

⑥ Place the filled jars on a rack in the preheated canner. Process for 10 minutes once the water has returned to a boil.

⑦ When the processing time is up, carefully remove the jars from the canner using a jar lifter.

⑧ Cool sealed jars. Check seals. Remove screw bands. Label. Store.

Jams, Jellies,
Preserves,
and
Marmalades

Basic Plum Jam
Makes about 8 half-pint jars

> 4 pounds tart plums (2 quarts chopped)
> 6 cups sugar
> 1½ cups water
> ¼ cup lemon juice

① Preheat the canner, sterilize the jars, and prepare the lids.

② Wash plums. Remove pits and chop.

③ Combine the plums, sugar, water, and lemon juice in a tall, heavy saucepan.

④ Bring slowly to a boil, stirring occasionally, until sugar dissolves. Then boil rapidly until thick, about 20 minutes. As the mixture begins to thicken, stir frequently to prevent scorching.

⑤ Test for doneness — 220°F on a thermometer or when the jam sheets off the spoon (see page 165).

⑥ Pour into the jars, leaving ¼-inch headspace. Wipe the rims of the jars with a clean, damp cloth. Adjust the lids as the manufacturer recommends.

⑦ Place the filled jars on a rack in the preheated canner. Process for 10 minutes once the water has returned to a boil.

⑧ When the processing time is up, carefully remove the jars from the canner using a jar lifter.

⑨ Cool sealed jars. Check seals. Remove screw bands. Label. Store.

Basic Apple Jelly
Makes 4 to 5 half-pint jars

3 pounds apples	3 cups sugar
3 cups water	2 tablespoons lemon juice

① Wash the apples. Chop into small pieces but do not peel or core. Combine with water in a heavy-bottomed saucepan and boil for about 25 minutes, or until apples are quite soft.

② Pour into a damp jelly bag or colander lined with a double thickness of damp cheesecloth. Allow the juice to filter out into a bowl.

③ Allow the juice to sit overnight so that any sediment can settle to the bottom. Do not squeeze fruit pulp, as the resulting juice will not be clear.

④ When you are ready to make the jelly, preheat the canner, sterilize the jars, and prepare the lids.

⑤ Combine 4 cups of the clear apple juice with the sugar and lemon juice in a tall, heavy-bottomed saucepan. Stir to dissolve the sugar.

⑥ Bring rapidly to a boil. Continue boiling until jelly reaches 220°F on a jelly thermometer or sheets off the spoon (see page 165).

⑦ Remove from heat and skim off any foam that formed during boiling.

⑧ Pour into the jars, leaving ¼-inch headspace. Wipe the rims of the jars with a clean, damp cloth. Adjust the lids as the manufacturer recommends.

⑨ Place the filled jars on a rack in the preheated canner and process for 10 minutes once the water has returned to a boil.

⑩ Cool sealed jars. Check seals. Remove screw bands. Label. Store.

Jams, Jellies,
Preserves,
and
Marmalades

Orange Marmalade
Makes about 7 half-pint jars

6 large oranges
2 medium lemons
6 cups water
About 6 cups sugar

① Wash the fruit. Remove the peel from the oranges and thinly slice. Chop the orange pulp. You should have 4 cups of thinly sliced peel and 4 cups of orange pulp. Thinly slice the lemons. You should have 1 cup of slices.

② Combine the fruit, peel, and water in a tall, heavy-bottomed saucepan. Heat to a simmer and continue to simmer for 5 minutes. Remove from the heat, cover, and let stand for 12 to 18 hours.

③ Return the mixture to the stove and cook over medium heat until the peel is tender, about 1 hour.

④ Preheat the canner, sterilize the jars, and prepare the lids.

⑤ Measure fruit and liquid. For each 1 cup of fruit mixture, add 1 cup of sugar. Bring to a boil, then cook rapidly until marmalade reaches 220°F or sheets off the spoon (see page 165), about 25 minutes.

⑥ Pour hot marmalade into the jars, leaving ¼-inch headspace. Wipe the rims of the jars with a clean, damp cloth. Adjust the lids as the manufacturer recommends.

⑦ Place the filled jars on a rack in the preheated canner. Process for 10 minutes once the water has returned to a boil.

⑧ When the processing time is up, carefully remove the jars from the canner using a jar lifter.

⑨ Cool sealed jars. Check seals. Remove screw bands. Label. Store.

Oven-Baked Apple Butter
Makes 5 to 6 half-pint jars

> 6 pounds apples (about 12 apples)
> 2 cups cider or water
> Sugar, honey, or maple syrup to taste
> Cinnamon (optional)
> Ground cloves (optional)

① Wash the apples and cut into small pieces, leaving skins and cores. Combine with the cider or water in a large heavy saucepan. Bring to a boil and boil until apples are soft, about 30 minutes.

② Purée apples in a hand-cranked strainer or food mill.

③ Heat oven to 200°F. Place mixture in shallow baking dish and bake, uncovered, in the oven until quite thick, 6 to 8 hours. Stir occasionally.

④ Shortly before cooking time is up, preheat the canner, sterilize the jars, and prepare lids.

⑤ Sweeten apple butter to taste. Add a little cinnamon and cloves, if desired.

⑥ Pour into the jars, leaving ¼-inch headspace. Wipe the rims of the jars with a clean, damp cloth. Adjust the lids as the manufacturer recommends.

⑦ Place the filled jars on a rack in the preheated canner. Process for 10 minutes once the water has returned to a boil.

⑧ When the processing time is up, carefully remove the jars from the canner using a jar lifter.

⑨ Cool sealed jars. Check seals. Remove screw bands. Label. Store.

Jams, Jellies,
Preserves,
and
Marmalades

CHAPTER 9

Troubleshooting

IT'S VERY DISCOURAGING to have anything go wrong
when you are preserving food. Following directions carefully
is the best way to avoid failures, but many factors can lead
to a failure. The following commonly asked questions should
help to solve — and prevent — many potential problems.

Freezing Questions

Q Should all vegetables be blanched before freezing?

A In the past, it was thought that all vegetables, except onions and peppers, should be blanched before freezing. However, we have discovered that some vegetables are best not blanched, including beans, young broccoli, chopped peppers, and sliced summer squash. Corn in husks, whole tomatoes, and chopped onions also can be frozen without blanching.

Q My frozen green beans are slimy and tough. How can I overcome that?

A Green beans should not come in contact with water any more than necessary. Best results are obtained by freezing green beans that are unblanched or have been blanched in boilable bags for 6 to 8 minutes. They should be cooked by steaming or frying.

Q When do you start counting time when you blanch vegetables?

A When blanching in boiling water (immersion blanching), timing is started as soon as water returns to a boil. If it takes longer than 2 minutes for the water to boil, you have blanched too much at once. Reduce the amount of vegetables in the next batch. Steam-blanch timing starts as soon as the cover is placed on the pan. Microwave blanching begins when you press the start button.

Troubleshooting

Q What is the best way to freeze sugar snap peas?

A Sugar snap peas should be steam-blanched for 3 minutes and tray-frozen. For the best cooked flavor, stir-fry sugar snaps.

Q Is it safe to freeze fruit without sugar?

A Yes. Sugar does not function as a preservative when freezing, but it does help to maintain color and texture.

Q Can I use artificial sweeteners in place of sugar for freezing fruit?

A Yes, since sugar isn't used as a preservative in frozen food. However, artificial sweeteners do not help the fruit maintain taste and texture as sugar does. To use artificial sweeteners, follow the directions on the package.

Q Why is my fruit sometimes mushy when thawed?

A If fruits are frozen slowly, large ice crystals form and rupture cell walls, causing mushy fruit. For best results, freeze quickly and serve just as ice crystals are disappearing.

Drying Questions

Q Why did my dried food become moldy?

A There are several possible reasons, all related to moisture. Perhaps the food was incompletely dried, or the container was not airtight, or the food was dried at too high a temperature, allowing the outside to harden before the inside moisture could escape. Prevent this in the future by testing the food within 1 week of drying. If signs of moisture appear in the food or in the jar, re-dry the food at 140°F until dry.

Q How can I prevent my fruit from sticking to the drying trays?

A Spray trays with vegetable cooking spray. Also, gently lift food with a spatula after 1 hour of drying.

Q Why are there brown spots on my dried vegetables?

A The temperature in your oven or dehydrator was too high.

Canning Questions

Q Sometimes my canning jars do not seal. Why?

A Jars that come with mayonnaise, peanut butter, or commercially packed pickles may not fit the canning lids properly. Other reasons for unsealed jars are dented or rusty screw bands; nicked or cracked jars; handling lids with greasy fingers; not screwing bands on tightly enough; food, seeds, or herbs caught between the jar and the lid when sealing or when liquid is lost from the jars during the processing; or insufficient heat during processing.

Q What causes jars to crack in the canner?

A Jars may crack if they are overfilled. Using a metal instrument or table knife to expel air will weaken the bottom of jars, causing them to fall off during processing.

Q Must glass jars be sterilized by boiling before canning?

A If the jars are to be processed for more than 10 minutes — as for most fruits and tomatoes — then sterilizing is not necessary. But be sure jars and lids are clean, and prepared according to manufacturer's directions before sealing jars.

Q Why is liquid lost from jars during processing?

A Loss of liquid may be due to packing jars too full. Failure to release air bubbles before sealing the jar will force out liquid when it begins to boil.

Q Should lost liquid be replaced?

A No. Never open a jar and refill with liquid; this would let in bacteria and you would need to process again. Loss of liquid does not cause the food to spoil, though the food above the liquid may darken.

Q How can I tell if my canned food is spoiled?

A The signs of spoilage are bulging lids, broken seals, leaks, change in color, foaming, unusual softness or slipperiness, spurting liquid when the jar is open, mold, or bad smells. If any of these signs are noted, do not use the food. Discard it where animals and humans cannot find it. Be mindful that some spoilage, such as botulinum toxin, may not exhibit obvious signs. That is why it is so important to follow proper processing procedures.

Q What makes canned food change color?

A Darkening of food at the tops of jars may be caused by oxidation due to air in the jars or by too little heating or processing to destroy enzymes. Over-processing may cause discoloration of foods throughout the containers. Iron and copper from cooking utensils or from water in some localities may cause brown, black, and gray colors in some foods. When canned corn turns brown, the discoloring may be due to the variety of corn, to the stage of ripeness, to over-processing, or to copper or iron pans.

Q Is it safe to eat discolored foods?

A The color changes noted above do not mean the food is unsafe to eat. However, spoilage may also cause color changes. Any canned food that has an unusual color should be examined carefully before use.

Q Is it safe to use home-canned food if the liquid is cloudy?

A Cloudy liquid may be a sign of spoilage. But it may also be caused by the minerals in hard water or by starch from overripe vegetables. If liquid is cloudy, boil the food for 15 minutes before serving. Do not taste or use any food that foams during heating or has an off odor.

Q **What causes an accumulation of black material on the underside of some lids?**

A Natural compounds in some foods cause deposits to form on the underside of lids. Unless the jar had been sealed and then became unsealed, this deposit is harmless. Do not use a jar of food that has become unsealed.

Q **What causes a milky-colored film on the outside of my jars?**

A Hard water leaves a mineral deposit on the outside of jars. To prevent this add ½ cup vinegar to each cannerful of water in hard water areas.

Q **Is it safe to can food without salt?**

A In many cases, yes. Often, salt is used for flavor only and is not necessary for safe processing, as is the case with the recipes in this book.

Q **Is it all right to use preservatives in home canning?**

A No. Some canning powders or other chemical preservatives may be harmful.

Q **Is processing time the same no matter what kind of stove you use?**

A As long as water in a boiling-water-bath canner remains boiling throughout the processing time, the processing times are the same.

Q **Is it safe to can foods in the oven?**

A No. Oven canning is dangerous. Jars may explode. The temperature of the food in jars during oven-processing does not get high enough to ensure destruction of spoilage bacteria in vegetables.

Q **Why do tomatoes sometimes float in the jar?**

A Tomatoes that are raw-packed have a natural tendency to float. In addition, tomatoes may float if they are overripe, if they are packed too loosely, or if they are overprocessed.

Troubleshooting

Q Why is open-kettle canning not recommended for fruits and vegetables?

A In open-kettle canning, food is cooked in an ordinary kettle, then packed into hot jars and sealed without processing. The temperatures obtained in open-kettle canning are not high enough to destroy all the spoilage organisms that may be in the food. Spoilage bacteria may get in when the food is transferred from kettle to jar.

Q Is it safe to can overripe tomatoes in a boiling-water bath?

A Overripe tomatoes may be too low in acid to be safely canned by these methods. To be sure that the acid content is high enough (a pH rating below 4.5), add ¼ teaspoon of powdered citric acid per pint (½ teaspoon per quart), or 1 tablespoon lemon juice per pint (2 tablespoons per quart) before processing.

Q Why do the canning lids pop off when I can tomato juice that was liquefied in a blender?

A Blenders incorporate a great deal of air into the vegetables they liquefy. The juice should be heated to boiling and simmered 5 minutes to exhaust that air before canning. Juice and purées from hand-cranked strainers should be handled the same way.

Q Why can't I use my microwave oven for making jam?

A You can, but the results aren't guaranteed. When making microwave jams and jellies, it's important to use a recipe developed specifically for the microwave. It's even better to use a recipe developed for your particular microwave. Microwave jams and jellies boil over easily, so be sure to use a very deep bowl for cooking the product. You may not save any time in the process. Most recipes make such small quantities that canning is not necessary, since the resulting pint or half-pint can be stored in the refrigerator. For long-term storage, freezing or boiling-water-bath canning is necessary.

CHAPTER 10

Quick Harvest Meals

I HAVE TWO PIECES OF ADVICE for making harvest meal-times easier: Incorporate the vegetables you are processing into your meals, and have plenty of basic foods in the freezer ready to convert into instant meals.

A harvest dinner can be as simple as an attractive platter piled high with fresh vegetables. Serve a spicy peanut dipping sauce on the side and the whole family will be happy. Your just-picked vegetables also make quick and healthful pasta dishes and soups. For nights when you want something heartier, take lasagna or meatballs out of the freezer. While your main dish is warming, prepare a delicious vegetable side.

Instant Meals

AS WINTER SLIPS INTO EARLY SPRING, prepare extra meals to tuck away in the freezer for harvest-time dinners without hassle. You can freeze ahead dishes from recipes in this chapter, as well as individually frozen hamburg patties, beef and chicken stocks, and stew bases, crêpes, piecrusts for quick meat pies or vegetables quiches, and favorite casseroles.

To save time in meal preparation, incorporate the vegetables you are working with into your meal plan for that day or the following day. For example, if you are canning or freezing spaghetti sauce, plan a spaghetti dinner. Remove from the freezer the number of servings of Freezer Meatballs (page 196) or frozen, cooked ground beef that you need, or brown some fresh beef. While the meat is heating in a pan of spaghetti sauce, prepare the pasta, and you have an almost instant dinner.

Diced Meats: The Basis of Eleven Quick Meals

A SUPPLY OF DICED, cooked poultry, beef, pork, and ham frozen with their cooking broths can be the basis of a variety of different meals. Tender cuts can be roasted, cooled, diced, and packed with broth made from pan juices; less tender cuts should be simmered.

Roasts of beef, pork, ham, veal, chicken, and turkey up to 12 pounds can all be prepared by slow cooking in the oven — while you are busy elsewhere. To do so, prepare your roast as usual; do not stuff roasting chickens or turkeys. Early in the morning, roast the meat at the normal roasting temperature for 30 minutes. Reduce the oven temperature to 185°F (150°F for medium-rare roast beef and 200°F for a 10- to 12- pound turkey) and roast, uncovered, for 8 to 10 hours. The meat will be perfect for supper, and if you are a little late, it won't overcook.

Pot roast can be prepared the same way, adding vegetables if desired. Roast the meat covered for ½ hour at 375°F, reduce the temperature to 185°F, and roast 8 to 10 hours. Add seasonal vegetables, and you have a complete meal and enough leftovers to freeze for some instant meals.

Packages containing 2 cups of meat covered with broth will give you the greatest versatility. Here are just a few ideas for using these meats. I'm sure you will come up with more of your own.

* Combine with soup stock and seasonal vegetables for a hearty stew.
* Stir-fry with vegetables; add walnuts for variety.
* Make into hash.
* Cream chicken with new peas and carrots; serve over hot biscuits.
* Make sandwiches, salads, quiches, and casseroles.
* Mix with homemade Indian Relish (page 148), and serve on hamburger rolls.
* Mix with homemade Chutney (page 148), and serve over rice or noodles.
* Add to cooked vegetables and stock, thicken with flour, and top with a crust or biscuits for a quick meat pie.
* Make chow mein.
* Mix with vegetables and eggs for a quick stove-top frittata.
* Mix with rice and vegetables for stir-fried rice.

Quick
Harvest
Meals

Freeze-Ahead Recipes

THE FOLLOWING RECIPES are for foods that can be prepared in advance to save meal preparation time during the busy harvest season. Serve part the day you make it, and freeze the rest. Most are basic recipes that later can be used to create a variety of nourishing and delicious dishes using the sauces and vegetables you are preserving.

To save preparation time and energy, defrost frozen foods in the refrigerator overnight unless otherwise specified.

Preparation times given for all recipes in this chapter are based on using a food processor, blender, and electric mixer when preparing foods. If you do not use these appliances, be sure to add additional time. Also, when I added up the total work time, I did not include cooking, baking, and chilling times when I was free to perform other tasks.

3-in-1 Chicken Recipe

Makes 24 servings

This recipe takes about 2 hours (plus cooling and freezing time) to prepare, but you will have many delicious meals in your freezer.

12	pounds chicken fryer parts
1	tablespoon salt
1	large onion, cut in chunks
3	cups unbleached flour
3	cups crushed cornflakes
1¼	teaspoons baking powder
5	teaspoons salt
1	tablespoon garlic powder
1½	teaspoons dried tarragon leaves
1½	teaspoons dried chives
1½	teaspoons parsley flakes
3	eggs
¾	cup cold milk
2	teaspoons onion powder
	peanut oil for frying

① Place the chicken in a large kettle with the salt and onion and water to cover. Bring to a boil, and simmer for 20 minutes.

② Turn off the heat, and cool the chicken in the cooking broth (about 2 hours).

③ Drain chicken well, discard onion, and save the stock for soup.

④ While the chicken is cooling, mix the flour, cornflake crumbs, baking powder, and seasonings in a large shallow bowl. Set aside. Blend the eggs, milk, and onion powder in a second shallow bowl. Set aside.

⑤ In a large, heavy skillet or electric frying pan, heat 2 inches of oil to 380°F. Dip the chicken pieces in the egg mixture and then in the flour mixture. Fry until tender and golden brown on all sides. Remove the chicken from the frying pan, and drain on paper towels. It takes about 1½ hours to fry 12 pounds of chicken.

⑥ Cool completely (about 1 hour).

⑦ Tray-freeze for 12 hours.

⑧ When the chicken is frozen solid, package in large freezer bags to be used as needed.

Fried Chicken

Place frozen chicken parts on a well-greased baking sheet, and heat, uncovered, in a preheated, 400°F oven for 30 to 45 minutes. (Time depends on thickness of the chicken parts.)

Polynesian Chicken

While 8 pieces of chicken are heating in the oven as directed above, sauté 1 to 2 cups of vegetables (carrots, broccoli, onions, peppers) in 1 tablespoon of cooking oil until tender. Add 2 cups of homemade Chutney (page 148) and heat through. Remove the cooked chicken from the oven, and top with the vegetable-chutney sauce. Return to the oven and bake an additional 10 to 12 minutes. Serves 4 with rice.

Barbecued Chicken

While 8 pieces of chicken are baking as in the directions given with the Fried Chicken, sauté 1 medium diced onion in 1 tablespoon oil until tender. Add 1 cup homemade Ketchup (page 156), 1 teaspoon honey, 1 tablespoon prepared mustard, 1 teaspoon salt, 1½ tablespoons cider vinegar, ½ teaspoon Worcestershire sauce, and ¼ teaspoon hot pepper sauce. Simmer for 20 minutes. When the chicken is heated through, top with the barbecue sauce and return to the hot oven for an additional 10 to 12 minutes. Serves 4.

Ratatouille

Makes 10 to 12 servings

Ratatouille is a great harvest dish. It makes good use of eggplant, zucchini, and peppers. You can serve it hot or chilled, or freeze it for enjoying later. In fact, making ratatouille is an excellent way to preserve extra eggplant and zucchini. You can serve this as a vegetarian main dish, or serve it as a topping for rice or pasta. For nonvegetarians, stir in 2 to 3 cups of chopped, cooked turkey or chicken.

6 tablespoons olive oil
3 onions, chopped
4 garlic cloves, minced
2 medium to large peeled eggplants, diced
2 green peppers, diced
2 red peppers, diced
8 medium zucchini, sliced
6 tomatoes, chopped, or 1 (28-ounce) can whole peeled tomatoes, drained and chopped
1 (6-ounce) can tomato paste
1 cup water
1 cup chopped fresh parsley
1 cup chopped fresh basil
Salt
Pepper

① In a large Dutch oven, heat the oil. Add the onions, garlic, eggplant, and peppers, and sauté until the vegetables are limp, about 8 minutes.

② Stir in the zucchini, tomatoes, tomato paste, and water. Heat to boiling. Reduce heat to medium, cover, and cook for about 15 minutes.

③ Add herbs, and salt and pepper to taste. Continue cooking, uncovered, for about 10 more minutes.

④ Cool for 1 hour, stirring often.

⑤ Package in meal-size portions in straight-sided containers. Leave 1-inch headspace. Label. Freeze.

To serve: Ratatouille served over rice or pasta makes a quick weeknight supper. Simply defrost and heat. Serve with grated cheese on top and a fresh garden salad on the side.

Meatloaf
Makes 2 large or 4 small loaves

       3 pounds ground beef
       1 pound ground pork
       4 eggs
       2 large onions, cut in chunks
       6 slices bread, torn in small pieces
    1½ cups milk
      ¾ teaspoon dry mustard
       1 teaspoon garlic powder (optional)
    1½ teaspoons dried thyme
       4 teaspoons salt
      ½ teaspoon pepper

① Preheat the oven to 325°F. Place the beef and pork in a large bowl. Place the rest of the ingredients in a blender or food processor. Blend until smooth. Pour this over the meat, and mix thoroughly. Divide into two 9- by 5- by 3-inch loaf pans, or four 8- by 4- by 2-inch pans.

② Bake for 1½ hours (in large pans) or 1 hour (in small pans).

③ Remove the loaves from the oven. Drain excess fat. Cool completely.

④ Remove the loaves from the baking pans and wrap for the freezer. Label. Freeze.

To serve: Defrost overnight in the refrigerator and serve cold, surrounded by fresh vegetables or in sandwiches. Or reheat in a 350°F oven for 20 to 30 minutes.

You can top meatloaf slices with Spaghetti Sauce (page 154), Sweet-and-Sour Sauce (page 148), or hot mashed potatoes covered with a slice of your favorite cheese. Slip the meat back into the oven until the cheese melts or the sauces are heated through.

Quick and Easy Lasagna
Makes 12 large servings

> 4 cups Spaghetti Sauce (page 154, or use your favorite recipe)
> 2 pounds cottage cheese
> 2 cups sour cream
> 1 pound uncooked lasagna noodles
> 1 pound mozzarella cheese, sliced thinly
> 1 cup grated Parmesan cheese
> 2 cups water

① Preheat the oven to 350°F.

② Line two 9- by 13-inch baking dishes with foil. Spread 1 cup of spaghetti sauce in the bottom of each dish. In a bowl, mix the cottage cheese with the sour cream. Layer the ingredients in the casserole dishes, beginning with the noodles, followed by the cottage cheese and sour cream mixture, then the mozzarella, ½ cup sauce, and finally the Parmesan cheese. Repeat 1 more layer, dividing the ingredients evenly between the casserole dishes. Pour 1 cup water around the sides of each dish.

③ Cover tightly with foil and bake for 1 hour. If both casseroles are to be frozen, remove from oven after 1 hour. If a pan of lasagna is to be eaten immediately, bake it uncovered an additional 15 minutes or until the noodles are tender. Let stand 15 minutes before serving.

④ Cool for 2 hours.

⑤ Freeze.

⑥ Remove the casserole from the baking dish. Wrap with freezer wrap or foil. Return to the freezer.

To serve: Return to a baking dish and defrost in the refrigerator overnight. Bake covered in a preheated, 350°F oven for 30 to 40 minutes. Let the lasagna stand 15 minutes before serving.

Freezer Meatballs
Makes about 100 meatballs

5	pounds lean ground beef
3	eggs
1½	cups quick-cooking oatmeal
¾	cup grated Parmesan cheese
3	large cloves garlic
2	large onions, coarsely chopped
1½	teaspoons dried oregano
2	tablespoons dried basil
2	teaspoons crushed red pepper
1	tablespoon salt
¾	teaspoon black pepper

① Place the beef in a large bowl. Put the eggs, oatmeal, cheese, garlic, onions, herbs, and spices in a blender or food processor. Purée until smooth. Add to the beef and mix thoroughly with your hands.

② Preheat the oven to 400°F.

③ Shape the meat mixture into 1-inch balls. Place on lightly greased, rimmed baking sheets.

④ Bake for 25 minutes at 400°F.

⑤ Cool at room temperature for 30 minutes. Drain fat.

⑥ Tray-freeze. When frozen, pack in large plastic freezer bags. Freeze.

To serve: For a 15-minute supper on the day you are making Jan's Spicy Spaghetti Sauce (page 154), ladle some sauce into a saucepan, add the desired number of frozen meatballs and simmer until the meatballs are heated through, about 15 minutes. Meanwhile, prepare some quick-cooking vermicelli. Serve with a fresh garden salad.

Another quick meal can be made by heating the meatballs in spaghetti sauce, and serving them on hamburger rolls for hot meatball sandwiches.

Chili

Makes 25 servings

    4 pounds lean ground beef
    2 tablespoons vegetable oil
    3 cups diced onion
    3 cups diced green pepper
    8 cups cooked, drained kidney beans
    2 quarts canned tomatoes (page 92)
 1½ cups tomato paste
    1 cup water
    2 tablespoons chili powder
   ½ teaspoon cayenne pepper
   ½ teaspoon paprika
    3 large bay leaves, crushed finely
       Salt and pepper

① Brown the beef in oil. Add the remaining ingredients.

② Simmer uncovered until thick, about 2 hours. Stir occasionally.

③ Cool for 1 hour, stirring often.

④ Package in meal-size portions in straight-sided containers. Leave a 1-inch headspace. Label. Freeze.

To serve: Defrost the chili overnight in the refrigerator, or run cold water over the container to remove the frozen chili and reheat in the top of a double boiler.

Serve with diced raw onion and grated Parmesan cheese, or serve in taco shells topped with diced onion, lettuce, and shredded cheddar cheese.

Baked Beans
Makes 10 to 12 servings

A cold-weather favorite to fill you up after long days of har-
vesting or preserving, baked beans are a sweet New England
tradition. They pair well with all types of greens and casual meat
dishes, such as hamburgers or hot dogs.

 2 pounds navy pea beans
 4 quarts cold water
1½ cups brown sugar, packed
 2 teaspoons dry mustard
 1 teaspoon salt
 ½ teaspoon pepper
 ½ teaspoon hot pepper sauce
 ¼ cup tomato paste
    Boiling water
12 small onions, thinly sliced
12 slices fresh (uncured) bacon

① Rinse the beans with cold water. Place in a 10-quart kettle. Add
4 quarts of cold water. Let stand overnight.

② Cook the beans in the water they were soaked in. Cover the
kettle; bring the beans to a boil. Then lower the heat and simmer
until tender. Skim off the foam as it rises to the top.

③ Drain the beans. Preheat the oven to 325°F.

④ Line two 2-quart baking dishes with foil. Divide the beans
between the 2 baking dishes. Put half of the brown sugar, dry mustard, salt, pepper, hot pepper sauce, and tomato paste in each dish.
Cover the beans with boiling water. Stir well. Top with onions, then
fresh bacon slices.

⑤ Bake, uncovered, for 4 hours, adding water as necessary.

⑥ Cool at room temperature for 1½ hours.

⑦ Freeze for 12 hours.

⑧ Remove the frozen beans from the baking dishes. Wrap extra well with freezer wrap or foil. Label and return the packages to the freezer.

To serve: Defrost frozen beans in the refrigerator. Place the foil package in a baking dish. Bake, uncovered, in a 325°F oven for 1 hour. Add a small amount of boiling water, if necessary. Or place the frozen casserole back into a casserole dish. Put in a 325°F oven and bake covered for 1 hour, uncover, and bake another hour. Add boiling water if necessary.

Cold baked beans can be mashed, with raw onion to taste, for a sandwich filling. This mixture is delicious served on rye bread with a spicy mustard.

Harvest-Time Dishes

IN THE THICK OF PRESERVING VEGETABLES, you can save time by cooking a dinner based on the vegetable you are processing. Base the whole meal around the vegetable, or use a vegetable dish to supplement some of the casseroles and other goodies you have tucked away in the freezer for busy days.

Here are a few of my favorite vegetable recipes.

Magic Crust Broccoli Pie
Makes 4 to 6 servings

2 cups chopped cooked broccoli
1 cup chopped cooked ham
¾ cup shredded cheddar cheese
½ cup unbleached flour
⅛ teaspoon salt
¾ teaspoon double-acting baking powder
1 tablespoon shortening
2 eggs
¾ cup milk

① Preheat the oven to 350°F.

② Layer the broccoli, ham, and cheese in a well-oiled 9-inch pie plate. Blend the remaining ingredients in a blender or food processor, or with an electric hand mixer. Pour over the cheese layer.

③ Bake, uncovered, for 40 minutes.

④ Let stand for 10 minutes before serving.

Vegetable Platter with Peanut Sauce
Makes 4 servings

Vegetables

    4 large carrots (scrubbed and peeled, if desired)

    4 medium potatoes, peeled and cut into chunks

    ½ medium head of cabbage, cut in wedges

    2 cups whole green beans

    1 medium bunch broccoli, separated into slender stalks

1½ cups water

Sauce

    ¾ cup peanut butter

    ¼ cup chopped peanuts

    ½ cup beef stock, bouillon, or water

    ½ cup light cream

    1 tablespoon lemon juice

    1 clove garlic, finely minced

    ¼ teaspoon crushed red pepper

① Prepare the vegetables: Bring the water to a boil in a large kettle. Add the carrots and potatoes. Reduce heat, and cook for 15 minutes.

② Add the cabbage, beans, and broccoli. Continue cooking until the potatoes are tender and the other vegetables are tender-crisp, about 15 minutes.

③ Drain the liquid, and keep the vegetables warm. Meanwhile, combine the sauce ingredients in medium saucepan, and cook over medium heat until heated through.

④ Arrange the vegetables on a large platter and top with the sauce.

Quick
Harvest
Meals

Cheese Stuffed Peppers
Makes 4 servings

4 large green peppers, seed pods removed
1 large tomato, scalded, peeled, and cubed
2 teaspoons fresh basil, finely chopped,
  or ½ teaspoon dried
¼ teaspoon salt
  Dash pepper or cayenne pepper
½ pound sharp cheddar cheese, cut in ¼-inch cubes
½ pound Swiss cheese, cut in ¼-inch cubes

① Bring 2 inches of water to a boil in a 4-quart kettle. Preheat the oven to 375°F.

② Arrange the peppers in a standing position in the kettle and par-boil for 6 to 8 minutes.

③ Drain the peppers. Place them standing upright in a lightly greased baking dish. Combine the tomato and seasonings and spoon into the peppers, dividing the filling evenly. Mix the cheeses together and stuff into the peppers, rounding off the tops.

④ Bake until the peppers are hot and the cheese is melted, about 20 minutes.

Spinach Surprise
Makes 6 to 8 servings

1	cup unbleached flour
¾	teaspoon salt
1¼	teaspoons baking powder
2	tablespoons shortening, melted and cooled
¼	cup milk
4	eggs
¼	cup fresh parsley, finely chopped
½	cup diced onion
1½	cups cooked spinach, well drained
¼	cup grated Parmesan cheese
4	ounces Monterey Jack cheese, cut in ¼-inch cubes
1½	cups cottage cheese
½	teaspoon salt
2	cloves garlic, minced finely

① Preheat the oven to 375°F.

② Grease a 12- by 7½-inch baking dish.

③ Mix the flour, ¼ teaspoon of the salt, baking powder, shortening, milk, 2 of the eggs, parsley, and onion. Beat vigorously for 20 strokes. Spread the mixture in the baking dish. Combine the remaining 2 eggs with spinach, cheeses, salt, and garlic, mix well, and spoon evenly over batter mixture.

④ Bake until set, approximately 30 minutes.

⑤ Let stand for 5 minutes before serving.

Quick
Harvest
Meals

203

Cucumbers in Dill Sauce
Makes 4 servings

  4 slender 5- to 6-inch cucumbers
½ cup plain yogurt
½ cup sour cream
  1 tablespoon chopped fresh dill, or 1 teaspoon dried dill seed
¼ cup chopped green onions

① Peel the cucumbers and slice thinly.

② Combine the remaining ingredients and pour over cucumbers. Mix well.

③ Cover and chill in the refrigerator for 30 minutes.

Harvest-Time Acorn Squash
Makes 4 servings

    2 medium acorn squash
       Boiling water
    3 tablespoons butter, melted
    ¼ cup packed brown sugar
    ¼ teaspoon cinnamon
    ¼ teaspoon salt
    ⅛ teaspoon nutmeg
    1 cup prepared applesauce
    2 teaspoons butter

① Preheat the oven to 375°F. Bring water to a boil in a teakettle.

② Wash the squash, cut in half lengthwise, remove seeds and stringy fibers. Place the squash, cut side down, on a rack in a shallow baking pan. Pour in ½-inch boiling water. Cover the pan with a tight-fitting lid or with foil.

③ Bake for 30 minutes.

④ Remove the pan from the oven. Pour off the water, turn the squash cut side up. Combine the melted butter, 2 tablespoons of the brown sugar, and the spices. Spread over the edges of the squash pieces. Fill the centers with applesauce; top with the remaining brown sugar and the 2 teaspoons butter.

⑤ Bake until the squash is tender, approximately 15 minutes.

Quick
Harvest
Meals

Pesto Pasta

Makes 4 to 6 servings

For a more satisfying dish, add 1 to 2 cups of lightly steamed vegetables, such as broccoli, green beans, diced carrots, or a combination of vegetables, to the sauce.

3 tablespoons pine nuts, walnuts, or sunflower seeds
2 garlic cloves
½ cup herb paste (see page 126)
½–¾ cup grated Parmesan, Romano, or Asiago cheese
½–¾ cup extra-virgin olive oil
  Salt
  Pepper
1 pound pasta

① Begin heating salted water for the pasta.

② In a food processor or blender, grind the nuts. Add garlic and grind again. Add herb paste and cheese, and process very briefly. With the motor running, slowly drizzle in the oil until the mixture has a sauce consistency. Season to taste with salt and pepper. Set aside.

③ Cook the pasta according to the package directions. Drain. Immediately toss the hot pasta with the pesto. Serve at once, passing additional grated cheese at the table.

Pasta with Garden Salad Sauce

Makes 4 servings

This is delicious served with Fried Chicken (page 190).

- ¼ cup vegetable oil
- 1 medium green pepper, coarsely chopped
- 1½ cups coarsely chopped broccoli
- 1 cup coarsely chopped onion
- 1 large clove garlic, finely minced
- 2 large tomatoes, scalded, peeled, and chopped
- 3 tablespoons cider vinegar
- ½ teaspoon dried basil, or 2 tablespoons fresh basil, chopped finely
- 4 cups precooked pasta

① Put 3 quarts of water in a large pot and bring to a boil. Heat the oil in a large heavy skillet. Add pepper, broccoli, onion, and garlic to the skillet. Sauté the vegetables until tender-crisp.

② Add the tomatoes, vinegar, and basil. Cook for 2 minutes. Keep warm.

③ Drop the pasta into the boiling water. Return the water to a boil. Turn off the heat and let the pasta remain in the water for 1 minute.

④ Drain the pasta. Top with vegetable sauce and serve.

Quick
Harvest
Meals

Squash Bisque
Makes 6 to 8 servings

2	tablespoons butter
1½	cups diced onion
1	cup diced celery
1	cup chopped mushrooms
3	tablespoons chopped fresh parsley, or 1 tablespoon dried
¼	cup chopped green pepper
¼	cup chopped sweet red pepper
2	cups mashed, cooked winter squash
2	cups chicken stock, bouillon, or water
	Dash of cayenne pepper
	Salt
	Pepper
1	cup milk
¼	cup light cream

① Melt the butter in a 4-quart saucepan. Sauté the onion, celery, mushrooms, parsley, and green and red peppers until the onions are limp but not brown, about 5 minutes.

② Add the squash, stock, cayenne pepper, and salt and pepper to taste. Simmer for 15 minutes.

③ Add the milk and cream, and reheat just to boiling. Serve.

Dutch-Style Green Beans
Makes 4 servings

3 slices bacon, diced
1 medium onion, diced
2 teaspoons cornstarch
¼ teaspoon salt
¼ teaspoon dry mustard
½ cup chicken broth or water
1 tablespoon cider vinegar
1 tablespoon brown sugar
2 cups chopped cooked green beans
1 hard-boiled egg, chopped

① Sauté the bacon in a large skillet until crisp. Remove from the pan. Add the onion to the pan drippings and sauté until tender.

② Blend in the cornstarch, salt, and mustard. Stir in the broth and cook, stirring constantly, until thickened.

③ Stir in the vinegar and sugar; add the beans and heat until bubbly. Serve with bacon and chopped egg.

Quick
Harvest
Meals

Lettuce and Green Pea Soup

Makes 4 to 6 servings

     2 cups fresh peas (frozen peas may be substituted)
     8 cups shredded crisp head lettuce
     ½ cup sliced green onions
     1 clove garlic, minced finely (optional)
     2 cups chicken broth or bouillon
     1 teaspoon sugar
     1 teaspoon salt
     ½ teaspoon dried chervil
       Dash pepper
    1½ cups light cream

① Shell the peas.

② In a heavy 4-quart Dutch oven, combine the lettuce, peas, onions, garlic, if using, and broth. Cover the kettle and bring the contents to a boil. Reduce the heat and simmer for 15 minutes.

③ Pour half of the mixture into a blender and purée until smooth. Pour into a bowl. Put the balance of lettuce mixture in the blender with the sugar, salt, chervil, and pepper. Purée until smooth.

④ Return all the lettuce mixture to a saucepan if you are going to serve it warm and mix well, or mix well in a bowl to serve cold. Add the cream. Reheat or chill. Serve.

Fifteen Creamed Vegetable Soups
Each soup makes 4 servings

Many delicious, fresh summer soups can be made from vegetable purées. These soups can be served hot or cold, as appetizers or as the main meal. Either way, they are quick and satisfying. They take just 10 to 15 minutes to make with prepared purées from fresh cooked, canned, or frozen cooked vegetables. On the chart on the following pages, you will find suggested ingredients and amounts for 15 different creamed vegetable soups. In each case, to make the purée, combine 3 cups of cooked vegetables with 1 cup of stock or water and purée in the blender. Purées for soup are best made with chicken stock, but vegetarians may wish to use water and increase the seasonings for extra flavor, or use vegetable stock.

① Sauté the onion in butter until tender but not brown.

② Place in the blender with half of the purée and half of the cream or milk. Blend until smooth. Pour into a saucepan (or bowl, if to be eaten chilled). Blend the remaining ingredients; add to first half. Stir well. To serve warm, reheat just until piping hot.

③ To serve cold, chill for several hours.

> tip ❋ As with most soups, these are better if made ahead so that flavors can blend. All the soups can be garnished with chopped chives, parsley, croutons, bacon bits, yogurt, sour cream, or grated Parmesan cheese.

Simple Recipes for 15 Creamed Vegetable Soups

	INGREDIENTS	
3 Cups Vegetable Purée of:	Onion	Butter
Beans, Green or Yellow	¼ cup	1 tablespoon
Beets	½ cup	1 tablespoon
Broccoli and Cauliflower	½ cup	2 tablespoons
Cabbage	¼ cup	1 tablespoon
Carrots	¼ cup	2 tablespoons
Corn	⅛ cup	2 tablespoons
Cucumbers	½ cup	2 tablespoons
Greens	¼ cup	2 tablespoons
Peas, Green or Sugar Snap	½ cup	2 tablespoons
Summer Squash	1 cup	2 tablespoons
Tomatoes	½ cup	2 tablespoons
Winter Squash I	¼ cup	2 tablespoons
Winter Squash II	¼ cup	2 tablespoons

INGREDIENTS

Light Cream or Milk	Seasonings
1 cup	2 dashes Tabasco, ¼ teaspoon garlic powder, ½ teaspoon dried basil, salt and pepper to taste
0	¼ teaspoon garlic powder, 1 cup stock, 1 tablespoon lemon juice, ½ teaspoon celery salt, salt and pepper to taste; top with yogurt or sour cream
1 cup	4 ounces grated cheddar cheese, salt and pepper to taste
1 cup	½ teaspoon celery salt, salt and pepper to taste
1 cup	¼ teaspoon curry powder, salt and pepper to taste
1 cup	1 cup diced chicken, 1 tablespoon chopped chives, salt and pepper to taste
1 cup	salt and pepper to taste; top with yogurt or sour cream
1 cup	½ teaspoon cayenne, salt and pepper to taste; top with yogurt or sour cream
1 cup	4 ounces grated cheddar cheese, 1 tablespoon cooking sherry, salt and pepper to taste
1 cup	½ teaspoon dried tarragon, salt and pepper to taste
1 cup	½ teaspoon curry powder, salt and pepper to taste
1 cup	6 ounces diced American cheese, salt and pepper to taste
1 cup	½ teaspoon cayenne, salt and pepper to taste

Quick
Harvest
Meals

Eight More Harvest-Time Meal-Planning Tips

1 **Layered salad.** Layer up a make-ahead salad in a large bowl. Layer shredded lettuce, peas, green onions, cooked macaroni, chopped tomatoes, sliced cucumbers, chopped walnuts, and diced chicken. Make a creamy dressing of 1½ cups mayonnaise, ¼ cup light cream, and 2 tablespoons chopped chives. Pour the dressing over the salad but do not toss. Cover with foil or plastic wrap and chill for several hours or overnight.

2 **Slow cookers.** Slow-cooked meals are time- and energy-savers. To adapt your own favorite stew recipe to the slow cooker, triple the recommended cooking time for the low setting or double it for the high setting. When cooking vegetables in the slow cooker, parboil them 6 to 10 minutes before adding to the pot. Always place vegetables in the bottom of the slow cooker with the meat on the top. Reduce the amount of liquid in your stew or casserole by about one-third and reduce the seasoning by at least that much.

3 **Quick fillers.** Precook several servings of potatoes, rice, pasta, and hard-boiled eggs when you have an extra hour or so one day a week. They can be used for quick dishes during the week, such as potato salad, hash-browned potatoes, corned beef hash, creamed potatoes, soups, stir-fried rice, spaghetti, and egg salad.

4 **Pasta and rice.** Undercook pasta and rice by 4 to 5 minutes for baked dishes and 2 to 3 minutes for meals not requiring additional baking time. To reheat pasta for use with a quick sauce, bring lightly salted water to a boil, add pasta and return to a boil, drain, and add sauce. To reheat rice, place in a fine mesh sieve over boiling water and keep water simmering until rice is heated through, fluffing with a fork once or twice while heating; this just takes a few minutes.

5 **Quick main meals.** Cook a large roast, meat loaf, turkey, pan of lasagna, or stew on the Friday evening of a harvest weekend. It will serve as a quick main meal with the addition of a fresh salad, bread, and beverage — even if company drops in. Leftover meats and meatloaf can be used for sandwiches.

6 **Ready-cut vegetables.** Dice onions, celery, green peppers, and carrots. Place in plastic bags and refrigerate. This step saves time when preparing soups, salads, and casseroles. If all the vegetables are not used up in 4 to 5 days, freeze the remainder. These will not be good for fresh salads after they are frozen, but can be used in all other ways, including in stir-fried dishes and fried rice.

7 **Salad makings.** Tear salad greens (cut greens will turn brown around the edges when stored), wash, and spin dry; place them in plastic bags. They will retain their crispness up to a week. To keep tomatoes firm when sliced ahead, slice them vertically and store in a separate bag.

8 **Frozen casseroles.** Line casserole dishes with foil when making casseroles to be frozen. After the casseroles are frozen, they can be removed from the baking dish, freeing it for another use.

Quick
Harvest
Meals

215

Eight Freeze-Ahead Ideas

1 **Cheese.** Grate cheese for casseroles, pizza, and toppings, and store in your freezer.

2 **Toppings.** Prepare bread and cracker crumbs for toppings and coatings, and store in your freezer.

3 **Turkey.** Cook a large turkey with dressing. Slice the meat and cover with dressing and gravy. Freeze in meal-size portions.

4 **Individual servings.** Fix favorite foods or leftovers in individual foil or boilable-bag servings. Always chill any precooked foods before packaging. Refrigerate for use within a day or so, or freeze for longer storage. Hurry-up meals can be prepared by just popping foil packages in the oven or boilable bags in a pan of hot water. Little or no cleanup is necessary.

5 **Quick breakfasts.** Make extra pancakes and waffles and tuck some away in the freezer to give you a few extra minutes on summer mornings to package tray-frozen foods. The kids can fix their own breakfast by warming the waffles and pancakes in the toaster and topping them with fresh fruit, preserves, and a little yogurt.

6 **Ground beef.** Cook several pounds of ground beef; divide it into several containers to be tossed quickly into sauces and quick casserole dishes that require cooked ground beef.

7 **Quick desserts.** If your family loves desserts, spring is the best time to freeze a few extra fruit breads, whole grain and fruit bars, cookies, and sheet cakes for busier times. Bake sheet cakes and divide in 4. Do not frost. These can be used later as single-layer cakes or double-layer birthday cakes (two sections), or served with fresh fruit and toppings.

8 **Tray-freeze meats.** Meatballs, meat patties, fried chicken, and similar foods can be tray-frozen and packed in plastic bags. At mealtimes, take out the number of servings needed.

Appendix: *Handy Reference Charts*

FRESH FRUIT YIELDS			
Fruit	Fresh Weight	Frozen Pints	Canned Quarts
Applesauce	1¼–1½ lb.	1	
Berries	1 crate (24 qt.) 1⅓–1½ pt.	32–36 1	12–18
Cantaloupes	1 dozen (28 lb.) 1–1¼ lb.	22 1	
Cherries, Sweet or Sour	1 bu. (56 lb.) 1¼–1½ lb.	36–44 1	22–32
Cranberries	1 box (25 lb.) ½ lb.	50 1	
Currants	22 qt. (3 lb.) ¾ lb.	4 1	
Peaches	1 bu. (48 lb.) 1–1½ lb.	32–48 1	18–24
Pears	1 bu. (50 lb.) 1–1½ lb.	40–50 1	20–25
Plums and Prunes	1 bu. (56 lb.) 1–1½ lb.	38–56 1	24–30
Raspberries	1 crate (24 pt.) 1 pt.	24 1	12–18
Rhubarb	15 lb. ⅔–1 lb.	15–22 1	
Strawberries	1 crate (24 qt.) ⅔ qt.	38 1	

APPROXIMATE YIELD OF VEGETABLES FROM FRESH

Vegetable	Fresh	Frozen Pints	Canned Quarts
Asparagus	1 crate (12 2-lb. bunches) 1–1½ lb.	15–22 1	
Beans, Lima (in pods)	1 bu. (32 lb.) 2–2½ lb.	12–16 1	6–10
Beans, Snap, Green, and Wax	1 bu. (30 lb.) ⅔–1 lb.	30–45 1	12–20
Beet Greens	15 lb. 1–1½ lb.	10–15 1	3–8
Beets (without tops)	1 bu. (52 lb.) 1¼–1½ lb.	35–42 1	15–24
Broccoli	1 crate (25 lb.) 1 lb.	24 1	
Carrots (without tops)	1 bu. (50 lb.) 1¼–1½ lb.	32–40 1	16–25
Cauliflower	2 medium heads 1½ lb.	3 1	
Chard	1 bu. (12 lb.) 1–1½ lb.	8–12 1	3–8
Collard Greens	1 bu. (12 lb.) 1–1½ lb.	8–12 1	3–8
Corn, Sweet	1 bu. (35 lb.) (in husks) 2–2½ lb.	14–17 (whole kernel) 1	6–10 (whole kernel)
Kale	1 bu. (18 lb.) 1–1½ lb.	12–18 1	3–8

APPROXIMATE YIELD OF VEGETABLES FROM FRESH

Vegetable	Fresh	Frozen Pints	Canned Quarts
Mustard Greens	1 bu. (12 lb.) 1–1½ lb.	8–12 1	3–8
Peas (in pods)	1 bu. (30 lb.) 2–2½ lb.	12–15 1	5–10
Peppers, Sweet	⅔ lb. (3 peppers)	1	
Pumpkins	3 lb.	2	1
Spinach	1 bu. (18 lb.) 1–1½ lb.	12–18 1	3–8
Squash, Summer	1 bu. (40 lb.) 1–1¼ lb.	32–40 1	10–20
Squash, Winter	3 lb.	2	

DRYING HERBS IN A DEHYDRATOR
(SET DEHYDRATOR AT 110°F)

Herb	Dehydrator Drying Time	Herb	Dehydrator Drying Time
Anise	10–12 hours	Mint	6–8 hours
Basil	8–12 hours	Oregano	4–8 hours
Cilantro	6–8 hours	Parsley	6–8 hours
Dill, leaves	6–8 hours	Rosemary	6–8 hours
Dill seeds	4–6 hours	Sage	8–12 hours
Fennel, leaves	6–8 hours	Savory	6–8 hours
Fennel seeds	4–8 hours	Tarragon	6–8 hours
Garlic, chopped	6–8 hours	Thyme	6–8 hours
Marjoram	6–8 hours		

TIMETABLE FOR BLANCHING VEGETABLES FOR THE FREEZER			
Vegetable	Blanch in Boilable Bag, 4 bags at a time (in minutes)	Blanch by immersion or Steam, 1 pound at a time (in minutes)	Suitable for Freezing Unblanched
Beans, Green and Wax	6–8	3–4	Yes
Beets			No
Broccoli, Florets		3–4	Yes
Cabbage			Yes
Carrots, Sliced or Diced	8–10	3–4	No
Corn on the Cob	10	7–11	Yes
Corn, Whole Kernel	6		No
Greens	Stir-fry until wilted: 2–3 minutes		No
Peas, Green	4	2	No
Summer Squash	5		Yes

TIMETABLE FOR MICROWAVE BLANCHING VEGETABLES FOR THE FREEZER

Vegetable	Amount Vegetable	Amount Water	Microwave Blanch on High (100% power in minutes)
Asparagus	2 cups (1 pound)	¼ cup	3
Beans, Green and Wax	3 cups (1 pound)	½ cup	4
Broccoli	3 cups (1½ pounds)	½ cup	5
Carrots, Sliced or Diced	4 cups (1¼ pounds)	½ cup	3–4
Cauliflower	1 head, cut in florets (1 pound)	½ cup	4½
Corn on the Cob	4 medium ears	¼ cup	8–9
Greens	12 cups (1 pound)	⅛ cup	3½
Peas	2 cups (2 pounds)	¼ cup	2
Sugar Snap Peas, Snow Peas	2 cups (1 pound)	⅛ cup	2½–4

Procedure: Prepare the vegetable, chopping into even-size pieces.
Arrange in microwave-safe container. Add water. Cover.
Stir or rearrange halfway through blanching time. Chill, pack, freeze.

BOILING-WATER-BATH PROCESSING TIMES AT ALTITUDES OVER 1,000 FEET

Boiling-Water-Bath Canner

Fruit or Vegetable	Style of Pack	Jar Size	Process Time in Minutes		
			1,000 to 3,000 ft	3,001 to 6,000 ft	Over 6,000 ft
Apple Juice	Hot	Pt. or Qt.	10	10	15
Apples	Hot	Pt. or Qt.	25	30	35
Applesauce	Hot	Pt.	20	20	25
		Qt.	25	30	35
Apricots	Hot	Pt.	25	30	35
		Qt.	30	35	40
	Raw	Pt.	30	35	40
		Qt.	35	40	45
Cherries	Hot	Pt.	20	20	25
		Qt.	25	30	35
	Raw	Pt. or Qt.	30	35	40
Cranberry Sauce	Hot	Pt. or Qt.	20	20	25
Grape Juice	Hot	Pt. or Qt.	10	10	15
Nectarines	Hot	Pt.	25	30	35
		Qt.	30	35	40
	Raw	Pt.	30	35	40
		Qt.	35	40	45

BOILING-WATER-BATH PROCESSING TIMES AT ALTITUDES OVER 1,000 FEET

Boiling-Water-Bath Canner

Fruit or Vegetable	Style of Pack	Jar Size	Process Time in Minutes		
			1,000 to 3,000 ft	3,001 to 6,000 ft	Over 6,000 ft
Peaches	Hot	Pt.	25	30	35
		Qt.	30	35	40
	Raw	Pt.	30	35	40
		Qt.	35	40	45
Pears	Hot	Pt.	25	30	35
		Qt.	30	35	40
Plums	Raw	Pt.	25	30	35
	or Hot	Qt.	30	35	40
Rhubarb	Hot	Pt. or Qt.	20	20	25
Tomato Purée	Hot	Pt.	40	45	50
		Qt.	50	55	60
Tomatoes, Whole	Raw	Pt.	45	50	55
		Qt.	50	55	60

Note: To adjust processing times for jellied fruit products, add 1 minute to processing time for each 1,000 feet of altitude above 1,000 feet.

Preserving Equipment and Supplies

Allied Kenco
800-3556-5189
www.alliedkenco.com

Berry Hill Limited
800-668-3072
www.berryhilllimited.com

Canning Pantry
800-285-9044
www.canningpantry.com

CHEFS
800-884-2433
www.chefscatalog.com

Compact Appliance
800-297-6076
www.compactappliance.com

Cooking.com
800-663-8810
www.cooking.com

Creative Cookware
866-291-9199
www.creativecookware.com

Cumberland General Store
800-334-4640
www.cumberlandgeneral.com

E. D. Luce Prescription
Packaging
562-802-0515
www.essentialsupplies.com

Everything Kitchens
866-852-4268
www.everythingkitchens.com

Excalibur Products
800-875-4254
www.excaliburdehydrator.com

Electrolux Home Products
800-374-4432
www.frigidaire.com

Goodman's
888-333-4660
www.goodmans.net

Harvest Essentials
877-759-3758
www.harvestessentials.com

The Home Processor
770-535-7381
www.home-processor.com

Home Trends
888-815-0814
www.shophometrends.com

Homestead Harvest
877-300-3427
www.homesteadharvest.com

Jarden Home Brands
800-240-3340
www.freshpreserving.com

Kitchen Krafts
800-298-5389
www.kitchenkrafts.com

Kitchen Etc.
800-571-6316
www.kitchenetc.com

L.E.M. Products, Inc.
877-536-7763
www.lemproducts.com

Lehman's
877-438-5346
www.lehmans.com

Lemra Products
860-774-7024
www.lemraproducts.com

MacManiman Inc.
800-609-2160
www.dryit.com

The Mending Shed
800-339-9297
www.mendingshed.com

Nesco
800-288-4545
www.nesco.com

Pleasant Hill Grain
800-321-1073
www.pleasanthillgrain.com

Polsteins Home and Beyond
877-880-8877
www.homeandbeyond.com

Red Hill General Store
800-251-8824
www.redhillgeneralstore.com

Refrigerators, Freezers, & More
800-632-3142
www.refrigerators-freezers.com

SKS Bottle and Packaging, Inc.
518-880-6980 Ext. 1
www.sks-bottle.com

Sunburst Bottle Company
916-929-4500
www.sunburstbottle.com

US Appliance
877-628-9913
www.us-appliance.com

The Vermont Country Store
802-362-8460
www.vermontcountrystore.com

Williams-Sonoma
877-812-6235
www.williams-sonoma.com

INDEX

Page references in **bold** indicate charts; page references in *italics* indicate illustrations.

Other Storey Titles You Will Enjoy

The Big Book of Preserving the Harvest, by Carol W. Costenbader.
A revised edition of a classic primer on freezing, canning, drying, and pickling
fruits and vegetables.
352 pages. Paper. ISBN 978-1-58017-458-9.

Fix, Freeze, Feast, by Kati Neville and Lindsay Tkacsik.
Great recipes that start with a warehouse club tray pack of meat and end
with a freezer full of delicious meals, ready for thawing anytime.
256 pages. Paper. ISBN 978-1-58017-682-8.

The Gardener's A–Z Guide to Growing Organic Food,
by Tanya L. K. Denckla.
An invaluable resource about growing, harvesting, and storing for
765 varieties of vegetables, fruits, herbs, and nuts.
496 pages. Paper. ISBN 978-1-58017-370-4.

Making & Using Dried Foods, by Phyllis Hobson.
Step-by-step instructions for drying almost everything
with or without a commercial dehydrator.
192 pages. Paper. ISBN 978-0-88266-615-0.

Pickles & Relishes, by Andrea Chesman.
Quick-and-easy recipes to turn bumper crops into mouthwatering
pickles and relishes, using little or no salt.
160 pages. Paper. ISBN 978-0-88266-744-7.

Root Cellaring, by Mike and Nancy Bubel.
Suitable for city and country folks, with information on harvesting
and creating cold storage anywhere — even closets! — plus 50 recipes.
320 pages. Paper. ISBN 978-0-88266-703-4.

Serving Up the Harvest, by Andrea Chesman.
A collection of 175 recipes to bring out the best in garden-fresh
vegetables, with 14 master recipes that can accommodate whatever
happens to be in your produce basket.
516 pages. Paper. ISBN 978-1-58017-663-7.

These and other books from Storey Publishing are available
wherever quality books are sold or by calling 1-800-441-5700.
Visit us at *www.storey.com.*